CAMILLO'S GUIDE TO

Cutting & Styling

Written and illustrated by

Silvio Camillo

LONGMAN

Addison Wesley Longman
Edinburgh Gate, Harlow
Essex CM20 2JE, England
and Associated Companies throughout the world

First published 1996

British Library Cataloguing in Publication Data
A catalogue entry for this title is available from the British Library.

ISBN 0-582-27940-2

Library of Congress Cataloging-in-Publication data
A catalog entry for this title is available from the Library of Congress.

Produced by Longman Singapore Publishers (Pte) Ltd.
Printed in Singapore.

Contents

Foreword

Silvio Camillo, the man, the artist, touched you with the gentle worth of his nature and the richness of his artistry.

Yes, Silvio was an enlightened man. He formed shapes with hands that made hair stand in ecstasy. We watched in awe! He continuously renewed in us, respect for our craft.

I was twenty two years, searching; so were many others. We were drawn to Silvio. He taught the disciplines of his craftmanship, he encouraged us to reach for our dreams, to study our hands as the instruments of art, to visualize shape through the mirror. He was the original, who outstandingly created the difference in competition work.

Silvio was a man with few pretensions. I wonder if he knew how much he influenced fashion for those of us who took that direction. We learned from him balance, control, awareness of bone structure and, because of his quiet dominance, a sense of being.

Silvio, thank you for being.

With love and respect from all of us.

VIDAL SASSOON

Preface

This book is a comprehensive guide to the techniques and training required for hairdressing. It offers sound guidelines to the rules and principles which must always be applied, from the very beginning. A great deal of hard work is involved in becoming a hairdresser; many routine and sometimes rather dull tasks have to be learned and practised until they become automatic. There are no short cuts to success! When cutting and styling it is important to know what you are going to do from the start and you must adhere to a sound method of working. The text and illustrations in this book describe the basic methods that have guided me throughout my career in hairdressing. All directions given are intended for a right-handed person. Those who are left-handed must adapt the instructions where appropriate.

A scientific approach to an artistic profession is not always popular but, just as painting and sculpture require a basic knowledge of draughtsmanship and anatomy, so in hairdressing it is vital to have an understanding of hair structure and of skin and scalp problems. Once you have mastered the basic techniques you will be able to apply the rules and procedures and adapt them to suit any mood and to create whatever style is needed to keep up with the ever-changing face of fashion.

You too can become a professional hairdresser!

SILVIO CAMILLO

PART ONE

Introduction to Hairstyles and Hairdressing

one

The history of hairdressing

Throughout history, people have always had a fascination for hair. We are reminded frequently, through the works of artists, poets and writers, of the wondrous, magical and symbolic beauty of hair.

Myths and legends

Legendary tales from long ago became the foundation of myths and superstitions surrounding the evil power of witch's tangled locks, the magical allure of blonde tresses, and the dangerous fascination of fiery red-heads.

There is a legend from Eastern Europe about a group of beautiful women who believed eternal youth was theirs as long as they preserved and conditioned their beautiful blonde hair. If they lost even one hair, they died! Then there is the legend of Medusa whose hair had been changed into writhing serpents: anyone who saw this terrible sight was turned to stone. Instant death was also the fate of any man who caught a glimpse of the beautiful siren Lorelei combing her golden tresses beside the river Rhine. This powerful fascination with blonde hair still exists – princesses and fairy godmothers are predominantly cast as blondes.

It has been said that blonde hair not only symbolizes power, but also purity. Inevitably, hair became involved in a mass of superstitions and taboos, in many instances due to religious influences.

Redheads have the reputation of being distrustful and deceitful: both the Devil and Judas Iscariot, who betrayed Jesus, have been portrayed as having red hair.

English folklore states that if a woman's hairline grows low on the forehead and comes to a point she will become a widow – hence the expression 'widow's peak'.

The cutting and washing of hair is also associated with many superstitions. In some cultures it is believed that the spirit or soul dwells in the hair. In the Far East, certain cults would only cut hair to the sound of music which would drive the spirits away. Other cultures believed cutting the hair caused thunder and lightning.

Hairstyles in history

Despite these superstitions and religious influences people came to realise that hair could be cut, shaped and adorned in order to attract admiration, and throughout the world many interesting and curious shapes in hair styles developed – each race and culture defining its own particular characteristics in a different manner. These hairdressing styles were not only expressions of fashion, but in certain cultures were also a status symbol.

History books tell us that before the Romans came to Britain, the Ancient Gauls wore their hair long over their shoulders and the Druid Priestesses braided their hair with sacred plants.

In England, the earliest record of hairdressing was in the Saxon period, when the particular style of the time was two long plaits. These were worn by young maidens, possibly to indicate virginity as, once wedded, their hair was hidden and veiled by the traditional wimple.

In Norman times plaits were no longer hidden but became thickened with false hair, lengthened with tassels and intertwined with ribbons.

Richard the Lionheart, the dashing blonde hero of his time, set a trend for golden hair. To achieve this colour, yellow saffron mixed with other herbs and concoctions was used on the hair. Noblemen imitated their king, and the fashion was soon followed by women. Gilded locks which were plaited, wound into gold net bags and decorated with pearls, became the rage. These net bags, called cowls, were made stiffer and stiffer so that, by the 15th century, there were huge heart-shaped headdresses.

In Elizabethan times a high forehead was a mark of beauty and fashionable women plucked the hairline to improve on nature. Queen Elizabeth I enhanced her reddish hair with henna. She had short, light curls all over her head and also had many wigs made in the same style. During her reign she set the fashion for redheads, but when she died blondes came back into favour.

Wigs and hair ornaments

By 1660 only servants had their hair natural, wigs being the choice of the upper classes. This fashion lasted over a hundred years. Even then, human hair wigs cost a fortune and goat and horsehair were used frequently as a substitute in cheaper wigs.

Elaborate hair ornaments were made by craftsmen while artists and sculptors made designs and models before these were executed in hair. Women often adopted the hairstyles of famous personalities. For instance, ladies at the court of Charles II followed the style of his favourite, Nell Gwynn, who introduced ringlets. Here was a definite change! Sets of curls, specially wired to stand away from the face, were popularly known as 'heartbreak curls' and were sometimes looped with pearls.

Hair as art

Then came an era when hair as an 'art' came to the fore. Influenced by trends from many parts of Europe, society women took to being elaborately bejewelled and adorned with the many dramatic creations of their dressmaker and hairdresser. In the early 1700s Queen Anne favoured a hairstyle swept up off the neck and curled gently, with one ringlet hanging over the shoulder. The trend became popular throughout the century, both in England and in France, until eventually exaggerated hairstyles reached an all-time high in the late 18th century. There were fantastically ornate creations up to three feet high, decorated with feathers, flowers, fruit and, as we know from portraits, even large objects like ships.

Coiffure de la Belle-Poule

This amazingly elaborate style was the creation of the famous hair artiste Leonard. Marie Antoinette first wore it at a ball given at the Paris town hall.

Coiffure de Merveilleuse (Directoire)

Just before the French Revolution, hairstyles underwent a complete change, being replaced, effectively, by hats. At first the fashion was for small hats made of silk, but these in turn were replaced by the large, elaborate hats that were so popular during the Directoire period.

A hairdresser in the 18th century was indeed an artist, sculptor, designer, engineer and technician. Can you imagine what a tricky and intricate operation it was to prepare and execute the exquisite masterpieces of that period? It needed great ingenuity to balance such a design securely on the head of a lady going to a ball if it were to stay that way.

These exaggerated fashions came to a halt when Marie Antoinette of France became ill and was forced to have her hair cut off. Short hair then became the vogue and baby curls came into fashion. But change came again and again – hair was crimped and frizzed up (much like today's contemporary look) and was powdered blue, black or very white. About 1795 all women powdering their hair had to buy special licences costing a guinea a year, with special levies for unmarried daughters and servants! This tax became most unpopular and had disappeared by 1869. After that, only coachmen and footmen were powdered.

The Directoire Period

In the early 19th century a style was introduced throughout Europe that influenced the course of hairdressing greatly. This was the Directoire. This style was worn with the feminine high-waisted fashions and had a definite Grecian influence. It was gay, pretty and very feminine.

Victorian England

In England a somewhat sober period was introduced when Queen Victoria came to the throne. Femininity took on a passive demeanour. Circular plaits came into fashion, followed by Victorian ringlets. A centre parting with waves on either side then became the rage. There was also a return to the upswept hairdo, hair being piled high on top of the head, supported by delicate padding. Backcombing began to take over to give a foundation to these exaggerated hairstyles which, in turn, gave support to the full-brimmed, heavily trimmed hats of the Edwardian era.

Hair in the twentieth century

World War I brought a major change from the long, intricate hairstyles of the pre-war period. Suffragettes of all classes, voluntarily working in factories, influenced the change.

For the first time in centuries, hair was dressed in a neat and simple fashion and 'bobbed' hair was seen throughout the country. In the 1920s it became even shorter as a gesture of emancipation. 'Flapper' girls aped boys in figure and in fashion, and the famous 'Eton Crop' swept the country. This was an extreme cut, short at the back and sides, with longer lengths at the top and sometimes little tendrils of hair just in front of the ear, called kiss curls. The shingle or semi-shingle remained for those who did not want anything so extreme. The shingle involved a graduated cut to just above the occipital bone and the neckline was rounded and cut to a point (very reminiscent of some of the styles seen in 1986). The semi-shingle, as the name indicates, was a half version of the shingle, the graduation finishing just below the occipital bone.

Another major change was the flat cheek wave of the 1930s. This swept Europe, when Marcel Gratten revolutionized hairdressing techniques, with his invention of the Marcel Wave and the 'Iron Wave'.

The 'Eton Crop'

The Cheek Wave 1930

Prior to World War II, hairstyles reflected the femininity of clothes, as if rebelling against the eccentricity of the suffragette period and the Eton Crop. Severe cuts were 'out', but soft, flattering waved shapes, flirty curls and smooth glossy silhouettes with flat sides, were 'in'. During the war hair remained longer and was coiled into sausage curls or rolled up to form a halo around the head. For the next decade or so it was a period of recovery from the war years, rationing permits and the severity of controls. As industry recovered slowly, and fashion created a number of changes, so hairstyling began to assert itself also.

The 'Urchin Cut'   The 'Bubble Cut'

As the 'New Look' swept Europe, clothes and the cinema influenced hair fashion. Cutting became a visual art. The 'Bubble Cut' and the 'Urchin Cut' which had a definite Greek influence were the rage. Then there was the 'Poodle', and the 'Italian' which were very similar and introduced new terms and vocabulary to us. *Layering* was a general term used to describe shortening the hair length around the head in an organized pattern. *Feathering* meant reducing the thickness of the hair at the points, either with the scissors or the razor. *Slithering* meant using the scissors half open and, holding the points of the hair, slithering the scissors down towards the root to thin and reduce bulk. This could also be done with the razor. The razor was used a lot in cutting many of these styles, since they were short and had to be light and feathery, not blunt and clubbed. The 'Beehive', when it came in, was a definite throwback to the Edwardian and powdered fantasies with back-combing taking the place of horsehair pads and lacquer that of lard and glue.

Television and the cinema now began to exert a great influence on people as to the styles they wore. Raymond influenced the small-head look to counter the heavy back-combed looks that were being thrust upon women by popular TV programmes. Raymond was very successful and his styles were beautifully executed, neat and practical.

In the 1960s London took the world of fashion by storm. Mary Quant, an inspired new generation designer presented her collection of new designs: the 'Mini' was born and was an instant success. About the same time Vidal Sassoon launched his new look in hair and his precise, bobbed cuts ideally complimented the new looks in fashion and made women look very feminine. Vidal's influence on cutting impressed itself so much upon the hairdressing profession that even today his name is synonymous with geometric cutting.

Many of the cuts seen today are throwbacks to the bobbed and shingled era. 'Beautiful' hairdressing, that is artistic hairdressing, is now rare; the static, rather stunted, even garish, has taken its place in a world always hungry for change.

two

The structure and texture of hair

The difference in hair among races

Hair styling, perming and colouring were all established arts as long ago as 3000 BC. Hair designs throughout the world, though widely different, have often involved moulding, crimping, curling and colouring hair. Some historic methods were not dissimilar to those being used today. People used mud and herbs and made up their own recipes for colour using natural products such as certain barks of trees and shrubs.

The difference between racial types is illustrated clearly by nature of hair. There are three mains types of hair:

Mongoloid:
Hair of the Far Eastern countries, Japan, China, India, etc.
Characteristics – straight and coarse.

Negroid:
Hair of the races of African origin.
Characteristics – very woolly and tightly curled.

Caucasian:
Hair of the white races.
Characteristics – moderately wavy, curly or straight.

Hair colour tends to follow, geographically, that of skin colour. People who live in strong suns have a heavier quantity of melanin in the skin. This pigment is the natural protection against the sun and the ultraviolet rays and is the reason for their dark skin and hair. Red hair belongs to the blonde category and the lighter skin (or fair skin) that goes with it lacks melanin, hence the common combination of freckled skin with red hair.

The growth of hair

Whatever race or colour, all hair grows and develops in the same way. It is produced in tiny pockets in the skin called hair follicles.

Each hair follicle is formed before we are born. It develops initially from part of the epidermis, or outer skin, which is pushed down into the lower layer of the dermis where it joins with a small part of it to form a papilla or hairbulb. This is the nearest thing to a true root that a hair has.

Nourishment for growth comes from blood in the blood capillaries. Each hair is also connected to the nervous system. A nerve branch loops round the follicle and enters the papilla.

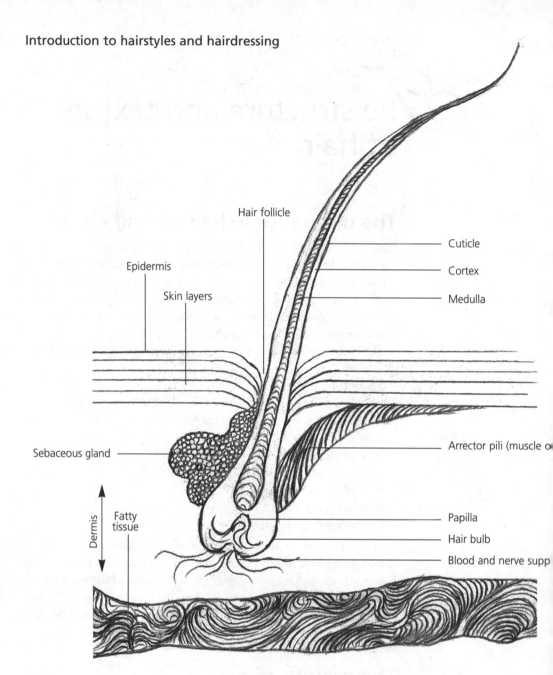

Hair in skin

Cell division occurs within the papilla and the new cells are pushed upwards into the follicle where they start to keratinize and harden. The keratinization or hardening process continues up the follicle until the hair emerges from the mouth of the follicle. As the cells push upwards, they take on one of three shapes, depending on which part of the papilla they were formed in – the cuticle, the cortex or the medulla. The cuticle is the outer layer of the hair, and has flattened scales overlapping in an upward direction. The inner layer is the cortex which is the strongest cell and most important,

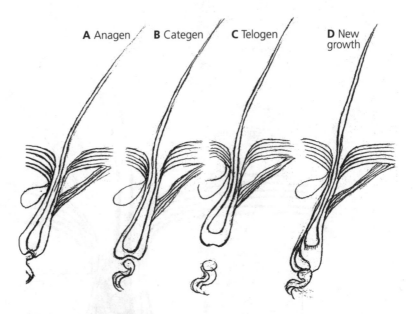

A Anagen   **B** Categen   **C** Telogen   **D** New growth

The growing stages of hair

A: Anagen – This is the normal active growing stage of hair. The growth varies from a few months to several years (average 4 to 6 years). It is during this period of growth that the length, thickness and texture of the hair is formed.

B: Catagen – This is the transition period when no further growth takes place, but at the papilla there is some shrinkage, where the hair bulb gradually detaches itself from the back of the follicle and starts to move upwards.

C: Telogen – This is the resting stage for about three months after which the follicle starts to lengthen and a new bulb and hair forms. If the old hair is still in the follicle it will be pushed out by the new hair as it grows upwards.

D: New growth – In this period the hair follicle has re-lengthened and the new growth forms and pushes old hair out.

for it also contains the cells of the colouring pigment. The middle cell is called the medulla

Lanugo hair or vellus hair contains no medulla. This is the hair seen on the premature or unborn infant, but it also describes the fine, downy, colourless hair that gives the female skin its soft velvety quality. Attached to each hair follicle is a sebaceous gland which produces oil, and a tiny muscle called the erector muscle or *arrector pili*.

Hair is not produced continuously by the hair follicle; there is an active growing period alternating with a resting period and, in between both, an intermediate period. When a hair has reached its normal life span the hair follicle starts to shrink and the hair will detach itself from the papilla. The detached end becomes round and starts to move up the follicle. At this stage the papilla will produce a new hair and the follicle returns to normal. These processes are called Anagen, Catagen, and Telogen as shown in the diagram above.

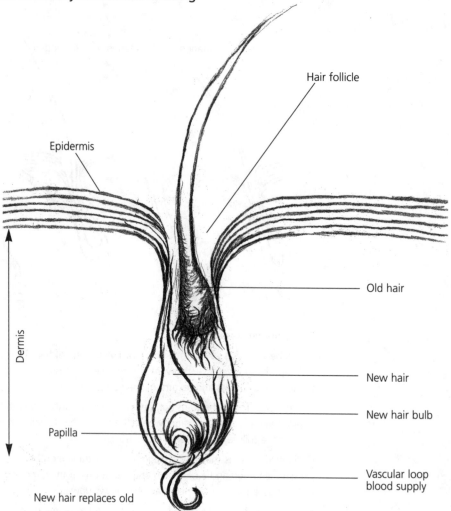

Hair follicle

Epidermis

Old hair

Dermis

New hair

New hair bulb

Papilla

Vascular loop blood supply

New hair replaces old

Hair is part of the body, as is the skin, and can reflect, like the skin, the general state of health of the body. Hair is defined as an appendage, or an outgrowth of the skin. It is found all over the body, with the exceptions of the palms of the hand and the soles of the feet. Its main function is protective. It is there to cushion the underlying area against a knock or blow. The eyebrows prevent perspiration running into the eyes, eyelashes guard against dust and irritants, hair in the nostrils prevent dust being inhaled, and in the underarms and within the pubic regions hair limits the effects of chafing and perspiration. Hair also acts as an insulator against cold or hot by trapping a layer of air close to the skin.

The lifespan of the long-term hair of the scalp or face is usually 4 to 6 years and that of the eyebrows and eyelashes 4 to 6 months. The average growth rate of a hair is approximately 13mm ($\frac{1}{2}$ inch) every 4 weeks.

Statistics state that an average healthy human scalp has an average of 100,000 hairs. Dark heads have an average of 108,000 and redheads and blondes about 90,000.

The study and science of hair is called trichology and diagnosis or diseases of the scalp and hair with associated treatments is carried out by a trichologist, who should be a qualified member of the Institute of Trichologists. Details about the main disorders, diseases and treatments are given in Chapter 15. *(See page 197)*.

The scalp and hair texture

Individuals have hair of different textures. It may be coarse, average, fine or baby fine. When treating hair during any hairdressing process it is necessary to understand the elastic nature of the scalp and hair. A moderately flexible scalp makes it relatively easy to control the hair with the comb when setting – it needs only some light pressure to make movement and curl. It is also quite easy to mould certain shapes into the hair while using heated irons, rollers or a hot brush.

A scalp that is easily flexible usually needs some increased pressure and tension to obtain any form of crispness within the shape being created, depending on the hair texture. The hardest type of head to work on is one that has a tight scalp, as it is very sensitive to the tough handling necessary to create a durable hairstyle. Some heads may necessitate the use of special gels or mousses to give extra support to the hair.

Hair types

Basically, there are four characteristic types of hair that we come in contact with in the salon. They are straight, wavy, curly and frizzy hair and each of these may have either a coarse, medium or fine texture. The hair type will usually indicate how it will respond to a change in shape. Hair that is average does not present any great difficulty in setting or styling with any of the heat procedures. Particularly coarse or fine hair can present problems as both will resist a change in form and shape, whether it is from curly to straight or vice versa. It is very difficult to permanently wave very fine hair and, likewise, coarse hair can be stubbornly resistant to change. For these types, lotions, winding procedures and rod widths have to be selected carefully in addition to the usual considerations regarding the thickness, condition and length of hair. Very fine hair, of course, should be treated with extreme care at all times. Wavy hair has a characteristic all of its own as it resists any change in shape. The setting must be exact, and the movement must be controlled when the hair is wet, otherwise it will revert back to its original form when dry. It may be necessary to consider 'relaxing treatment' to subdue the elasticity in the natural movement of the hair.

Length of hair

The length does not normally affect the texture or the general style of hair although in cases where the hair is too long and thick, the general condition and texture of the hair (from middle lengths to the points) may be in poor condition. It is usually dry and brittle, but a good general cut and re-shaping can transform it.

Patterns of growth

Hair tends to grow in various directions and follows distinctive patterns of growth. Listed here are some of the most common.

1. *A natural parting:* A pattern of growth, where the hair falls in two directions. Can occur anywhere on the head.
2. *Widow's peak:* Hair that grows to a point in the middle of the hairline on the forehead.
3. *Cow's lick:* A tuft of hair that grows upwards awkwardly.
4. *Whorl:* A circular growth of hair.
5. *A half whorl:* A half circular growth that grows either to the right or the left (sometimes mistakenly called a cow's lick).
6. There is occasionally an area on the one side of the head that has a thicker concentration of hair. This is known as the heavy side. The occurrence is rare.

three *Tools* of the trade and the basic cuts

Anyone taking up a sport for the first time is obliged to go through the initial stages of learning to play the game. Take golf, for instance, or tennis: in each of these games the most important point is learning how to handle the club or racket. Concentration on the alignment and the correct placing of the hands and fingers on the club is the starting point in golf. Coupled with studying a controlled swing and body movement, these are usually the frustrating but essential exercises in the first stages of learning golf. In tennis, too, you must learn how to grip the racket correctly before even striking a ball and then learn the knack of being balanced on the correct foot for making a forehand or backhand stroke or serving. In each of these examples the emphasis is on the hands, the fingers, the grip.

In hairdressing it is essential to appreciate, right from the very beginning, that your hands and fingers must feel comfortable when using the basic tools of the profession. Sensitivity of touch is extremely important to hairdressers, especially when using one of the first tools to be used, the comb.

Hairdressing tools

The comb

The comb is not just something to free tangles or to straighten unruly hair. It really does control hair! The fingers and fingertips control the action of the comb throughout the various stages of hairdressing. Only rarely is the comb held in the palm of the hand. The thumb, forefinger and middle fingers dictate the action of the comb. The actual fingertips control the motion of the comb. There are various techniques for working hair with a comb. On wet hair, for instance, the combing action feels different from that on dry hair or hair that has been processed in other ways. In the 'dressing-out' of a style, the touch of the comb must be very sure when manipulating the line that gives shape and movement in a hair style. The stroke of the comb must be light and delicate, yet sensitive to the texture and shape of the hair.

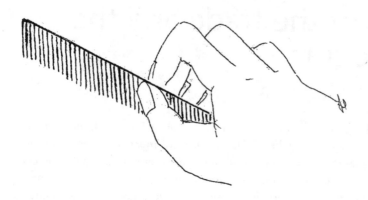

The Comb

The thumb, forefinger and middle fingers control the motion of the comb. The forefinger guides, the thumb steadies and the middle finger, with the others, supports the action. During the dressing of hair for example, the touch with the comb must be sure, yet the stroking on the hair light and delicate while still sensitive to creating a beautiful shape.

Combing wet hair

On wet hair, a little more pressure is needed to control any kind of manipulation. The illustration shows the change in the hold – the little finger moves over to the same side as the thumb to give an added strength to the grip. This grip is used mainly when the hair is being sculpted and moulded into a curved movement.

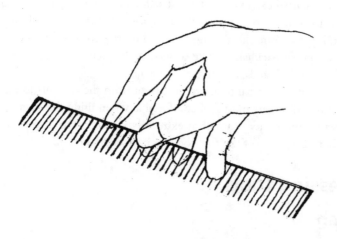

The tail comb is used to control the points and lift up sections.

The brush

Not enough thought is given to the correct handling of the hairbrush. It is not used merely to loosen hair or to eradicate the stiffness create by setting lotion. Don't just brush to loosen hair, brush to control the shape from the roots. The brush should be an extension of your arm and hand, providing extra help to create a shape from a mass of roller curl that needs to be controlled and subdued – otherwise the curl will control you! Hair that has not been brushed correctly will snarl and hang awkwardly.

The brush should be held firmly in the palm of the hand to give a secure grip with the thumb and forefinger well up over the back. By changing the position of the thumb and forefinger you can control the direction and pressure of the brush.

The brush illustrated was designed by the author and made by Comby Ltd, especially for brushing out after setting.

Special-purpose brushes are suitable only for what they were designed for, particularly those made for blow-waving. Brushes are made in all kinds of materials – plastic, metal, rubber, etc. Eventually the choice of a brush becomes very personal, as there are so many to choose from. For the purpose of dressing hair after a set, make sure the bristles (or the bristle-substitute fibres) are strong enough to pass through the hair and blend the roots together.

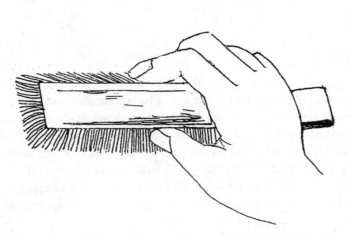

The brush

Hold the brush firmly in the palm of the hand with the thumb and forefinger well up over the back of the brush. Pressure from the thumb or forefinger will change the direction of the brush and control the hair movements as the bristles are pulled through the hair.

The scissors

The scissors must be chosen very carefully. Until you have had sufficient experience at cutting, it is wiser to select a medium sized pair of scissors that balance and feel comfortable in your hand. Later, when you are more proficient you may feel you need one or two pairs of scissors of various sizes.

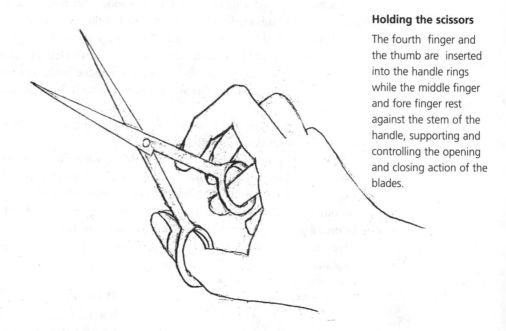

Holding the scissors

The fourth finger and the thumb are inserted into the handle rings while the middle finger and fore finger rest against the stem of the handle, supporting and controlling the opening and closing action of the blades.

The razor

The razor is a cutting tool that has its own particular technique and must be studied carefully. Unfortunately, a number of bad techniques have been handed down and some hairdressers are still using these out-dated methods. One in particular, is used in some modern salons, that of 'thinning', which is an old, out-dated term, emanating from an old-fashioned tool. This is the dog-stripper type razor, an instrument which has ordinary blades, fitted between two slats. It is used on hair with a crude, downward stripping stroke. This may be fine for the poodle parlour but certainly not for the professional hairdresser!

There are a number of well-designed razors on the market similar to a traditional razor. They have specially designed, replaceable blades with a guard that can be removed to facilitate a cut which requires a naked blade.

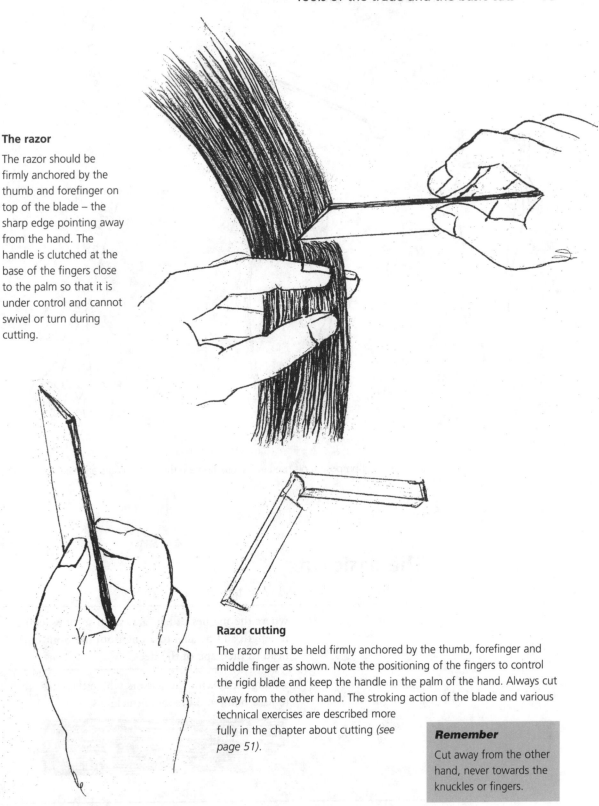

The razor

The razor should be firmly anchored by the thumb and forefinger on top of the blade – the sharp edge pointing away from the hand. The handle is clutched at the base of the fingers close to the palm so that it is under control and cannot swivel or turn during cutting.

Razor cutting

The razor must be held firmly anchored by the thumb, forefinger and middle finger as shown. Note the positioning of the fingers to control the rigid blade and keep the handle in the palm of the hand. Always cut away from the other hand. The stroking action of the blade and various technical exercises are described more fully in the chapter about cutting (*see page 51*).

Remember

Cut away from the other hand, never towards the knuckles or fingers.

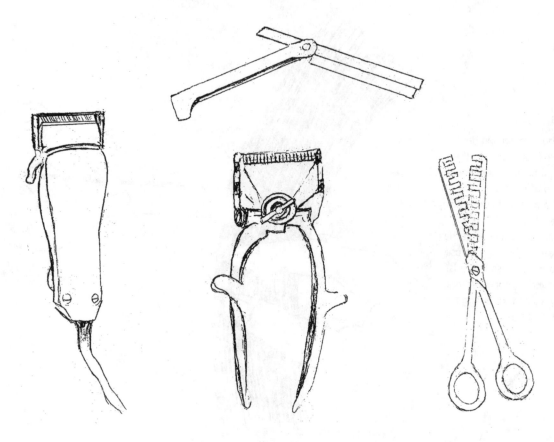

Other special-purpose tools used in hairdressing are thinning scissors and clippers.

The basic cuts

Some basic procedures and holds for cutting

Layer cut:	where the meshes of hair are cut in sections, equal in length and parallel to a line from the front of the head to the nape of the neck.
Club cutting or a blunt cut:	a straight cut with the scissors where the ends remain blunt and the same thickness.

Bevel cut:	this means cutting an even bevel on the points to finish the ends.

Point or taper cut:	when hair is cut to a point. This can also be described as the slither cut. As the name implies, it is a slither-like stroke with the scissors barely closed.

Scissors-over-comb cutting:	a way of producing a very short, even cut at the nape.

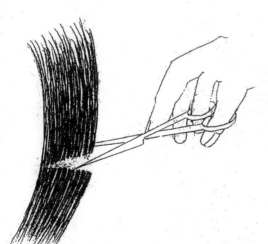

The forefinger, sensitive to the opening and closing action, is ready to control and steady the scissor blades during the cutting and shaping of the line.

The club cut

In the club, or blunt cut, the scissors cut the hair cleanly, leaving a thick, even edging at the ends.

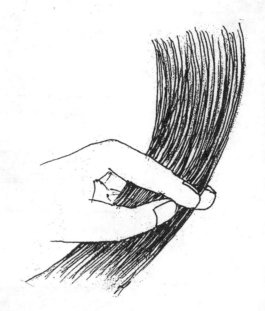

A change in the hold of the left hand facilitates a cut where the growth is a little awkward or the hair somewhat shorter, as at the nape of the neck. The right hand must adapt to this change by allowing the fingers to change the direction of the scissor angle. This will control the cutting of the ends.

The hair should be held firmly between the forefinger and middle finger of the left hand ready for cutting.

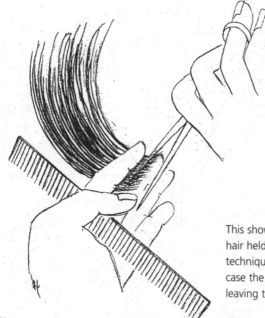

This shows another way of cutting the points with the hair held in the left hand with the palm upwards. This technique can be used to cut the whole head in which case the comb is conveniently held by the thumb, leaving the right hand free to cut.

Bevel cut

This shows a bevelling cut being executed on the ends. This is very similar to the club cut inasmuch as ends are cut evenly. The difference is that the fingers are turning the hair upwards slightly away from the head as the ends are trimmed, giving them a little graduation. The more the hair is held away from the head at an acute angle, the more the graduation.

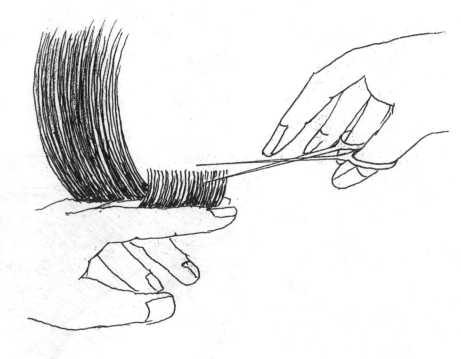

The slither cut or taper cut

This shows the sliding action of the scissors with the blades opened slightly on a mesh of hair. This technique of cutting is usually used to reduce bulk or thickness at the points to create a tapered effect. Used efficiently and with some skill, many varied effects are obtainable.

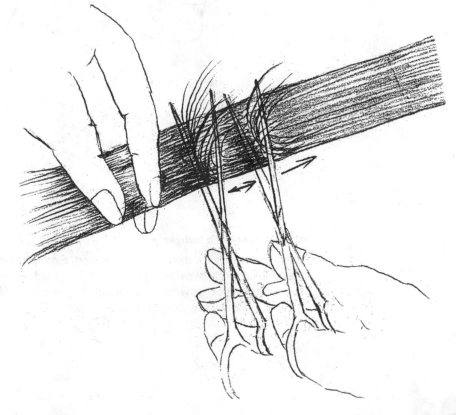

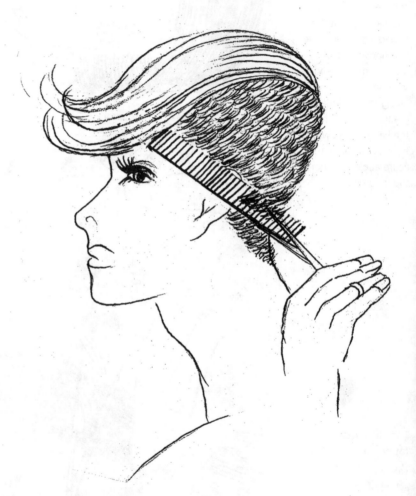

Scissors-over-comb technique

After hair has been cut short, an extremely short, even finish can be achieved by running the comb under the hair, pressing it flat against the head and then snipping off all the hair protruding from between the teeth with the scissors held flat against the comb. This is often used at the sides or nape in close-cropped styles.

haping hair

Finger control and shaping curves

Whatever the shape or line of a style, wet hair has to be combed and moulded to prepare the 'movement'. This is the basic groundwork before any curl or a roller is put in position, even if you are just scrolling a simple shape into the hair and leaving it to dry. This manipulating procedure is a vital technique for hairdressing process. Treated as an exercise, it teaches you how to 'move' hair and mould it very precisely in its wet state. You can scroll, sculpt and manipulate hair to suit any mood or facet of fashion,

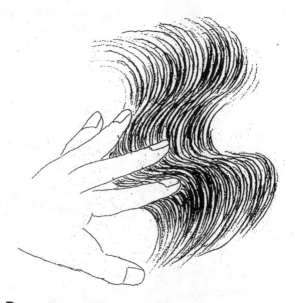

1. **Finger control and wet-hair shaping**
Outline the first part of a wave shape with the comb, then pause a moment while the middle finger of the left hand controls the movement with a firm pressure. Only then should the right hand change direction to create the next movement. The comb should always remain parallel to the curve and the finger. Use a series of strokes on each shape to ensure that the roots are controlled.

2. **Continuing the wave shape**
As the comb completes the next part of the movement the forefinger should be placed just underneath the next crest curving in the opposition direction. These movements provide the basis for setting, placing of a roller or creating a curl. A simple shape can also be moulded with gel and left to set. Practise these exercises on wet hair until you become proficient in creating beautiful movements.

> **Remember**
> As the middle finger changes its position, the comb changes direction.

This is a general exercise to be worked at with a comb on wet hair. Learn to evenly distribute the wet hair into a variety of different shapes as well as the one shown here. Create wide movements; circular shapes; one complete movement to one side; the hair combed back and shaped on each side of the head, and so on. Moulding the hair in this way will give invaluable practice and help you acquire good co-ordination of the hands and fingers when handling a comb.

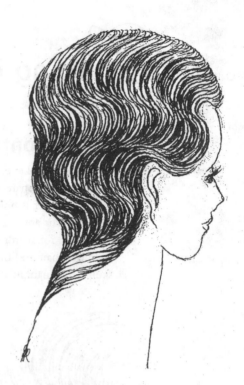

Rollers and pin-curls

There are various thicknesses of rollers, the choice being dictated by the kind of styling to be produced. Very large rollers are used to achieve a 'bob-like' look on longish hair. On other styles, a combination of different thickness and sizes may produce a curlier or bouncy look, with a controlled softness where needed.

Remember

There are various kinds of rollers that may be used. Different widths and sizes vary the tightness of the wind. The bigger rollers give a larger natural movement.

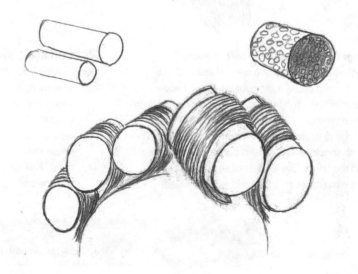

Clockwise and anti-clockwise curl

These are the two basic curls needed to produce a waved shape. There are many styles of presentation:

- thick, heavy curls with long stems to create dramatic look;
- a series of elongated movements with the points just turned under create a soft shape;
- smaller curls give a neat frothy look to the ends;
- light tendril shapes around the face to flatter it.

Clockwise Curl

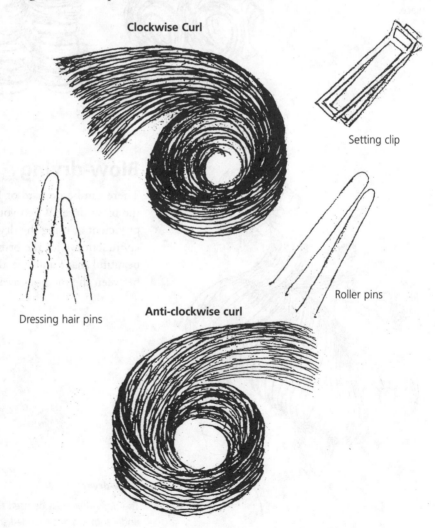

Setting clip

Roller pins

Dressing hair pins

Anti-clockwise curl

Reverse curling which creates a wave shape like this can be achieved by means of rollers or pin-curls. It is important to check the root control as there must be no root distortion when the pin-curler or roller is put in place.

Blow-drying

There can be no hard or fast rule about the use of the blow-dryer. When you have become proficient at using the dryer and know that in conjunction with the brush you can create a beautiful shape and line, then make a choice between the methods available.

Blow-dryer

The blow-dryer can be used to produce a soft turned-under look on this rounded shape.

The heated irons and hot brush

These are often used to create instant curl or bend in a style or cut. The hot brush, for instance, is useful in certain cases to create a special movement.

Sometimes when a blow-dryer has not produced enough bend on heavy, resistant hair, the irons can give extra bounce and add curl where needed.

(left) Heated irons can be used to produce an instant curl or bend to the hair around the face.

Heated irons can be used on longer hair to give additional bounce or curve to achieve a soft, natural look.

Hot brush

This is a very versatile tool that can be used in the same way as the heated irons. Carefully used, it can be a great asset.

There are, of course, many other items that could be mentioned such as clips and pins, special lamps for drying, the rods used in perming, and so on. Some of them will be described in later chapters, but here we have concentrated on the basic tools of the trade and the techniques associated with them that must be mastered.

Lubricants

Lubricants have to be used to treat hair that is to be processed by direct heat e.g. blow waving, hot brush, tongs, etc. In most instances the hair can be protected by the special lubricants formulated in conditioning lotions and creams. These condition and protect the cuticle of the hair during contact with heat and should be used before or during the appropriate hairdressing procedure. If blow-drying, coat the hair beforehand with a mousse, spray or lotion designed especially to cover the cuticle with a protective film, This also acts as a conditioner and will leave the hair soft and glossy.

five

In the salon

The stance

As a hairdresser, it is important to stand in a way that will enable you to work comfortably as well as allow you complete freedom of movement. Unless this is done the body will tire, muscles will go into spasm and posture could be permanently damaged.

While the basic guidelines described here are the same for everyone, individuals should adapt them to suit their own physique and attitude.

The three main points to remember are:
● How you should stand in relation to a head of hair before commencing any work.
● How to adjust your body, arms, legs and hands while working.
● How far away from the head you need to stand.

Taking each of these points in turn:

How you should stand
● Stand behind or in front of the client's head with your body weight distributed evenly between your feet.
● You should have a good balance with both feet evenly spaced apart in line with the hips and shoulders.
● The weight should be directed towards the balls of the feet rather than the heels.
● Do not tighten the leg or knee muscles – relax them. This keeps abdominal strain at a minimum.
● The arms frequently suffer and cause some tension in the shoulder and neck muscles, as they are often held incorrectly, particularly when perming. Hold the arms away from the body with the elbows outwards.
● Do not let the elbows creep downwards towards the body. This often happens when working on awkward heads that are perhaps too low or too highly placed. Remember to adjust the height of the client's chair.

Direction or line

● Never stand in one position all the time. It is impossible to work on the front of the head – or the side – while standing at the back. Move around the head. The hands and angles change, so your body must change with them.
● There are various tools that need to be used in perming, blow-drying,

using hot brush and irons, etc. You have to learn to adjust posture and body movement when using these tools. You will notice a difference!

Working distance

- There is one sure way of finding your correct distance. Stand behind the head, feet comfortably apart, and reach out to the head. If you are too near you will feel cramped; too far and you will feel awkward.
- To those whose height, or lack of it, might feel that these suggestions do not apply to them, be assured they do.
- To the taller: flex the knees a little more and position the feet a little wider. Also use a higher working position wherever possible. Avoid stooping and curb the tendency to allow elbows to creep downwards and inwards causing muscle drag and possible cramp.
  - Where lack of height is the problem, obviously the client's head must be lower.
  - Adapt commonsense rules to obtain a comfortable working position. For example, place a finger gently on the forehead to push the client's head backwards in order to reach the front of the head, or vice versa.

The danger of poor footwear must also be stressed. Floppy sandals, thonged footwear or heel-less shoes can be a menace. They give an illusion of being comfortable and casual but in fact are a hindrance, making it very difficult to acquire a good posture and balance. In the long term they are the largest contribution to leg trouble and the main cause of muscle drag and tiredness in the calves of the leg.

The correct posture

Your body should be erect with the weight evenly balanced; feet positioned slightly apart; elbows should be raised and away from the body.

Before beginning any hairdressing procedure always take care to adopt the correct body stance and to relax the shoulders and arms.

Whatever tools you are using, never let your elbows creep down and inwards to the body. Working uncomfortably in this manner will cause tension and create pull and cramp in the muscles of the arm. Keeping your body evenly balanced on the balls of the feet will help to avoid strain on the leg muscles.

Salon etiquette

One of the major aspects of salon etiquette concerns communicating with people. It is essential to be able to communicate agreeably with clients and good habits need to be cultivated. A sympathetic manner, courtesy and a pleasing appearance are important in the salon, especially to first-time clients. Traits and attitudes show through our features and disposition, and how you say something is as important as what you say.

Some people are nervous on their first visit and are acutely aware and sensitive to salon atmosphere. This is where professionalism plays a key role. Courteous manners and a warm smile help to relax new clients and make them feel valued. When you greet a client with 'Good Morning', look at them directly. Communication through the eyes will help to break the ice and relax your clients by giving them the assurance that you are concerned with them in particular, and in what they require.

A salon atmosphere which is affected in any way by tensions and contentions among the staff may cause a new client never to return; whereas friendliness, a sense of humour and a sympathetic approach help good relationships tremendously. Courtesy is needed at all times – even giving instructions to other members of staff should be done in a cheerful friendly manner.

Using the telephone

Because the person at the other end of the line cannot see you, your voice will convey your attitude. If you smile as you acknowledge a call it will help your voice to sound friendly and interested. Speak clearly and then allow the client what time they need to identify themselves and state their requirements.

Once you know these, and so that there can be no misunderstanding, repeat back the time and date of the appointment. Everyone answering a call on the telephone must know all the services that a salon offers. In addition, you should be familiar with the booking routines and how to deal with cheques, cheque cards, sales vouchers and the retail stock.

A receptionist should know each stylists' specialities and temperament in order to place a new client as well as possible. A hairdresser who can show friendliness and self-confidence should be selected. Once in the salon the client will be gowned, shampooed and passed over to her stylist who must take care of all her requirements until she leaves.

PART TWO

Basic techniques

six

*S*hampooing

The first hairdressing procedure that must be mastered is how to wash hair. Unfortunately, in some salons this is simply given to anyone who is available, but shampooing is an acquired technique and a vital part of a salon's service. A clear set of rules should be set up for the shampoo area as this is the first area that a new client experiences.

Hygiene, dress and etiquette

Hygiene and cleanliness must be evident throughout the shampoo area. Basins and all surfaces must be scrupulously clean and each client should be provided with fresh, spotless towels.

Remember that the client also sees you at close quarters, so your own hair and appearance must be faultless. You should make personal hygiene a priority, as body odour can be particularly offensive when shampooing: so too can baggy and sloppy clothes as they may annoy the person in the chair. Imagine being shampooed while the floppy, baggy sleeves of a fashionable jumper slaps you across the nose and face! Also beware of dangling, noisy bracelets and long necklaces which may get in the way.

Another source of irritation to clients which should be avoided is chatter and gossip or discussions about personal problems going on over their heads while they are at the basin.

Make sure that the hands and fingers have room to move around the head during a shampooing and rinsing procedure.

Shampooing procedure

Seat the client comfortably at the basin, making sure that the towel cushions the neck and protects it from contact with the cold, hard edge of the basin, and check that your hands and fingers can be manipulated around the head with ease during the shampooing process.

The hands should rotate on the head firmly but gently and the pads of the fingers should be used to feel the skin on the scalp, loosening the dirt and dust particles, while spreading the shampoo throughout the head and hair.

Three reasons for shampooing are:
1. To cleanse the skin and hair of any dirt and dust, grease or sebum and dead skin cells.

2. To prepare the client for any hairdressing procedure that needs clean hair such as permanent waving, cutting and styling. Hair that is clean will also set and blow-dry better.
3. To massage the scalp and improve blood circulation to the roots of the hair.

Massaging the scalp

A light massage can be given during the shampoo by using the pads of the fingers in smooth, rotating movements. Work from the front towards the crown and then the back of the head. Massaging increases the blood flow to the scalp which brings nourishment to the roots of the hair.

The two massage movements used in shampooing are known as *effleurage* and *pettrisage*.

Effleurage is a smooth, stroking action with the hands and pads of the fingers, executed firmly but gently in general massage. Used to improve blood flow and stimulate the function of the skin, it also acts to soothe and stimulate nerves and relax tensed muscles.

> **Remember**
>
> Only the soft, gentle, lighter movements should be used on the scalp during shampooing.

Pettrisage is a deeper, harsher, kneading movement used principally to break down adhesions, assist the elimination of waste products through the blood and increase a nutritious flow to the skin. There are a number of movements, such as pinching, pounding, squeezing and pressing, which can sometimes be very harsh.

Crown

Order of massage movements

1. Centre forehead to crown.
2. Receding point at temple to crown.
3. Side of head to crown.
4. Behind ear to crown.
5. Nape of neck to crown.

The shampooing procedure should always follow a certain pattern.

1. Thoroughly prepare the hair by checking that there are no pins or clips in the hair, then brush and comb the hair to remove any tangles.
2. This is the time to analyze and check the scalp and hair for any abnormalities or conditions, as well as assessing which shampoo is to be used or treatment given. No, shampoo or any treatment should be given if there is any doubt about a severe condition of the scalp or hair.
3. Before beginning to shampoo, stand comfortably with your body weight distributed evenly on both feet. Adjust the water flow and test the temperature of the water on the back of your hand. Check it again before applying it to the head.
4. Wet the client's hair and scalp thoroughly, then distribute the shampoo evenly through the hair, massaging the scalp with the rotating movements towards the crown as illustrated.
5. Make certain all parts of the scalp and nape of the neck are cleansed, taking care not to let the shampoo disturb make-up or splash near the client's eyes and ears. Use the hand to cup and protect the face from the spray during rinsing and be particularly careful of water trickling down the back of a client's neck while spraying the nape area.
6. Rinse thoroughly and apply shampoo for the second time. Repeat the massaging movements as before, making certain that all parts of the scalp have been cleansed well before the final rinse. Check the hair line and nape areas, making sure that the hair is free from dirt, shampoo or scum.
7. After rinsing, squeeze water from the lengths of hair by hand.
8. Use the corner of a towel to dab any surplus water from the ears and hairline.
9. Take the end of the towel from around the client's shoulders, wrap it over one ear and the front hairline towards the crown of the head. Then repeat the procedure on the other side, tucking the end in to resemble a turban.
10. Place a clean, dry towel around the client's shoulders and escort her or him back to a styling position.
11. Remove the towel and comb the hair as necessary, ready for the next hairdressing procedure.
12. Should the hair be tangled, use a tangle-freeing lotion or spray while combing as an aid to disentangle hairs and clumps that have knotted. Harsh combing on tangled wet hair can cause severe breakage along the hair shaft.

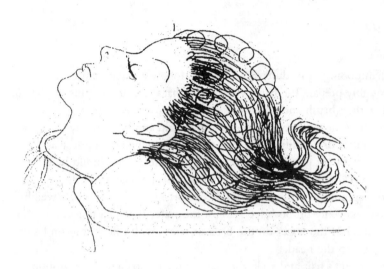

Backwash method

1. Hair should be brushed towards crown.
2. Thoroughly wet hair with water running in the same direction.
3. Distribute shampoo throughout the head.
4. Commence massage from centre forehead.
5. Continue with 2, 3, 4, working towards crown.
6. Rinse hair thoroughly in same direction.
7. Repeat whole routine
8. Rinse hair thoroughly (last rinse).
9. Wrap hair in towel making turban.
10. When at styling position take off towel.
11. Comb hair through.

Wrap the towel around the head like a turban after completing the final rinse.

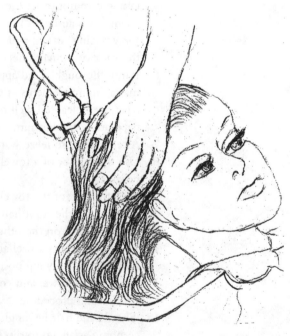

Be careful not to let the shampoo disturb the client's make-up or splash near the eyes. Use a cupped hand to protect the face from the spray during rinsing and be particularly careful of water trickling down the back of the neck when rinsing the nape area.

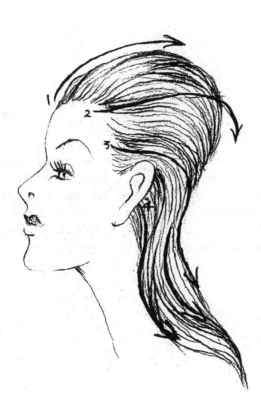

Combing wet hair

Short or medium length hair :

Start at front hairline and, assuming hair is free from tangle, comb from roots to points
using a No.4 comb taking the areas in the following order:

1. Start at centre front and comb hair towards nape
2. From the receding point at the hairline down to nape of neck
3. In front of ear at side of the head into the nape
4. From behind the ear into the nape

Long hair

Reverse the procedure starting with combing the points, then the mid length and only
when these are tangle free, comb through from the roots.

Shampooing for a perm

A thorough inspection of the scalp is necessary to make sure the skin of the scalp is free from cuts, scratches or abrasions of any kind. Should perm lotion (reagent) come into contact with sore or infected skin, the condition can be aggravated.

A soapless shampoo is generally used when shampooing before a perm, as this leaves the hair shaft clean, leaving no barriers that could prevent the lotion from penetrating the cuticle of the hair. Be gentle and remember that, if at all roughened by vigorous shampooing, some scalps become very sensitive to the perming process and the lotions involved.

Shampooing for a tint

First of all, wet the tinted hair around the hairline. Gently add a little shampoo which should be mixed with the tint around the hairline and massaged softly with the pads of the fingers. This treatment will gradually soften the tint around the skin on the hairline, enabling it to dissolve and be rinsed off, leaving no stain or residue of tint. After applying the tint, shampoo in the normal manner, then rinse well, thoroughly, several times, until the water runs clear.

Shampooing after using bleach

When the bleach has developed it is rinsed out of the hair using tepid water. Remember that the scalp can become very sensitive after a bleach, so take extreme care not to cause any discomfort. The hair should be rinsed until all traces of the bleach have been removed, especially if a toner is to be applied. When all traces of the bleach have been rinsed out, shampoo with care using massaging movements. While manipulating the hair, take care not to tangle the bleached hair. Be gentle!

The Structure of the head

To cut and style hair artistically and skilfully it is necessary to have a basic knowledge of the structure of the head and the main bones that dictate the curve and shape of the hair.

The skull

The skull dictates the shape of the head and is made up of eight curved bones which fit snugly together. The seams or joins between the bones are known as sutures. The diagram shows the location of all the bones and their names.

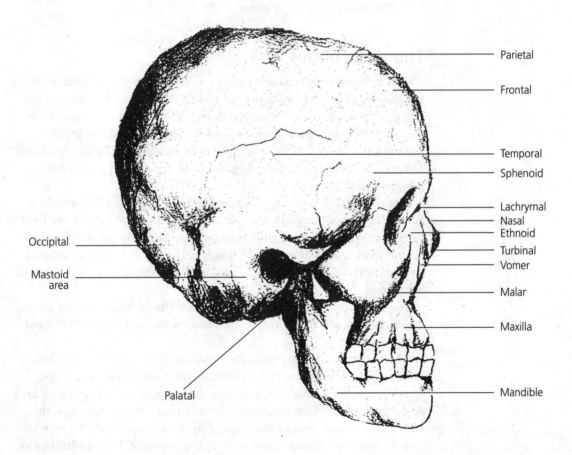

Bones of the skull

The scalp

The scalp is the covering of the upper part of the skull, from the forehead above the ears to the nape. It is composed of three layers of tissue which form the flexible part of the head covering. The underneath layer, called the epicranius aponeurosis, is connected to the bone with tissue. This layer is the muscular part of the scalp, known as occipito frontalis because of its connection with the frontal bones of the skull. The middle layer is a fatty layer and the outside layer is the skin from which the hair grows. These three layers together move as one.

The lower part of the head is the face, composed of fourteen facial bones: two maxillae, two turbinal, a mandible, two palatar, two malar, two nasal, two lachrymal, and a vomer.

The main bones

The main bones important to hairdressers are those in the occipital, temporal and mastoid areas. They influence the natural shape at the hair roots as the hair is swept away from the forehead across the temporal area, around the mastoid area or into the occipital area at the nape. These bones are of particular importance to those engaged in more advanced fashion work and competition hairdressing, since they dictate the controlling shape of the hair movement at the root.

The skull reveals how the curves of the bones underneath the scalp control the natural shape of the hair when it is moulded around the head in its wet state. These natural guidelines give the hair a curved shape and natural roundness before we even touch it. The classic wave is developed from this curved shape and is the basis of all the shapes and movements in hair design.

The feel of the head itself and the sides and the back dictate these natural guidelines that will enable you to cut beautiful shapes, fringes and tailored looks.

The parietal is the top part of the head. The frontal and temporal bones show up the slant of the receding hairline. These define a circular shape which acts as the natural line separating the top from the side and back areas. At the back of the skull, linking the mastoid areas behind each ear, is the occipital bone that controls the shape at the back of the head. Between the mastoid and immediately below the receding points of the front hairline are the side areas.

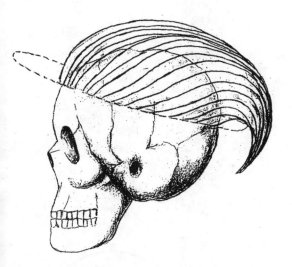

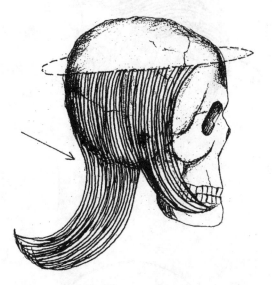

The top of the head is defined by the temporal, frontal and the parietal bones. This is a natural key to the 'circle guideline' at the top of the head - referred to later in cutting and setting.

At the back of the skull the occipital bone area (arrowed) dictates all movement at the nape of the neck. Between the mastoid process and the frontal bone are the sides.

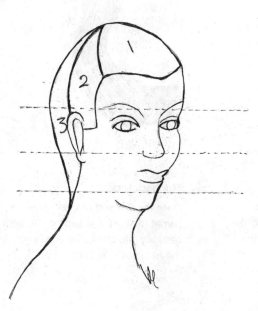

The 1-2-3 rule: top, sides and back

1. There is a top, two sides, and a back to every hairstyle. Let the shape of the head dictate the natural guidelines. The hairline, indicated at the receding points on the temple, on either side of the forehead, directs the imaginary circle towards the back of the head. The natural line automatically separates the top of the head, the side and nape movements. This natural line is a particularly good guideline when cutting a full fringe.

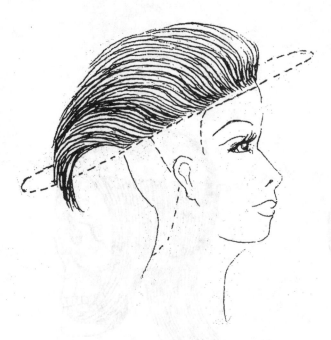

The 1-2-3 sectioning rule deliniating the top, sides and back.

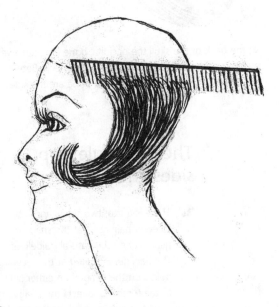

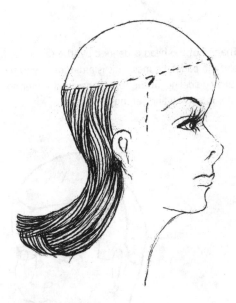

2. **The side section**

Starting at the natural line immediately below the receding point of the hairline, the comb should follow the slant of the hairline, mould the hair towards the back of the head then forwards, towards the face, to find the natural side movement. Correctly moulded, the hair will fall easily towards the cheeks.

3. **The back section**

Once the side sections have been moulded, the hair at the back and nape of the neck will fall naturally into place. The bone structure dictates the natural shape of this.

The start of a cut

Before beginning a cut it is necessary to spend some time assessing the head – looking for the natural fall of the hair; how it hangs from the head, especially round the ear and the occipital bone area at the back of the head. Feel the bulk and texture of the hair. The fall of hair around the head is controlled by the texture, length and, particularly, the growth direction. Dry hair obviously falls differently from wet hair. With a new client it is worth looking at the hair dry first.

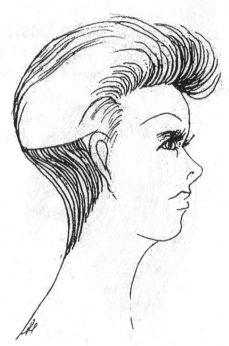

The hairline on the forehead often reveals variations in the hair follicles. Where the hairline has a strong natural root pull back off the face do not attempt to try any forward shape. The cut must be adapted with great care.

The occipital bone
The diagram shows the occipital bone area at the back of the head. The dipping shape of the skull into the nape of the neck creates a most effective movement in certain styling shapes. A study of the hair in the occipital area before cutting and setting will help to eradicate many errors that can occur at the nape. The growth direction of the root hair is often distorted here, sometimes growing awkwardly upwards, which means that cutting and setting procedures must be adjusted. There may also be a predominant swing to one side or the other. Where this happens, curve all the hair that way.

Check the density of the hair in certain areas and note the springiness of the root pull, especially around the forehead and nape where there are often distortions, usually called cow's-lick, or whorls, that will affect the fall of the hair. Sometimes it is necessary to leave hair a little longer in places to compensate for this. Look carefully at the eyes, nose and ears and look for any blemishes or unusual features: for this, the hair must be wet so that you can assess how the hair will fit around the head in the finished cut.

The basic cut: Stage One

The basic cut is dealt with in two parts: the outline, or perimeter, and the crown. Remember there are three areas to consider: the top, sides and back.

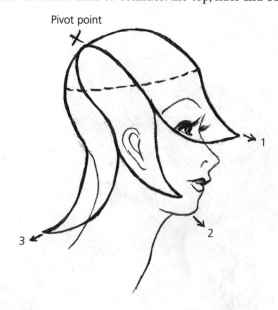

Comb the hair down to distribute it evenly around the head in preparation for the cut.

Pivot Point

The pivot point on the crown denotes the direction from which the sections are directed downwards and angled in preparation for cutting. The temporal section (the section on the front of the head) controlled by the two receding points on the temple (1) is combed towards the front above both eyes. The second section (2) on both sides of the head are combed and directed towards the face and chin. The back (3) follows a downward direction by the swing of the hair under the occipital bone. It is essential to use these guidelines when cutting lengths around the face.

The first part of the cut deals with the back and sides and the second part with the crown. Both parts are based on the 'circle method'. Imagine a circle framing the head. After the first part of the cut, this circle should be complete with the hair neatly bevelled when the hair is combed forward. The circle will change line and direction depending upon the kind of shape being executed. The second stage is to cut the final length with the hair combed back.

This basic cut can be made equally well with either scissors or a razor. The razor is an important tool to a hairdressing craftsman. It can be used very effectively at the nape of the neck where it gives results that scissors cannot achieve. It can also be used for a micro-laying technique called 'bodying' creating an invisible layering hidden within the bulk of the hair. Bodying technique should be carried out between the two stages of the cut after combing all the hair backwards from the face and before commencing the layering. (See page 56).

At the start of the cut the hair should be wet and combed towards the front.

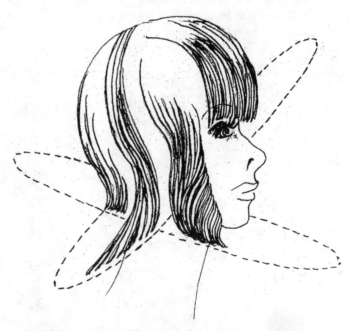

Establish in your mind the various finished lengths to be cut. The diagram illustrates how the angle of the cutting circle varies to suit the different lengths of a cut.

Cutting the outline with scissors

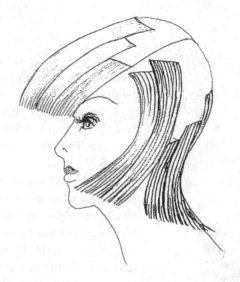

1. In this particular style the sides and nape hair are longer, while the front is cut into a fringe and the top is layered. Start by cutting an evenly balanced outline of the shape around the head. You should be cutting to an imaginary circle at each stage, keeping in mind the end result.

2. To cut the lengths around the head – the outer perimeter – you should always create guidelines in each section, as shown here, before combing all the bulk hair down. Make this a habit.

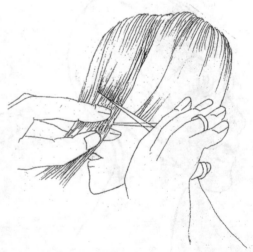

3. First, cut the front section. Stand in front of the client's head, holding the hair firmly between forefinger and middle finger. Remember the length you want to achieve: use the nose as a guide and never cut above the eyebrows.

4. Check that the hair is combed neatly with the fall of hair correctly directed towards the chin. Before making any final cut check the angle of the scissors; in this case they are pointing to just under the corner of the lips. For a guideline on the opposite side of the head, to get the correct angle you will have to imagine a line running from the lobe of the ear to the corner of the lips as the scissors will be pointing towards the nape.

5. To determine whether the swing on the cheeks falls equally on both sides, make sure every cut follows the same guideline – from just under the lips to points an equal distance from the lobe of each ear. This will give the exact line of cut every time.

Using the razor

A razor can also be used to cut the basic shape. This tool can be used to create some beautiful effects if used correctly. A razor cut will give a perfect bevel on fringe hair and nape hair and it will control certain shapes in hair better than a scissor cut.

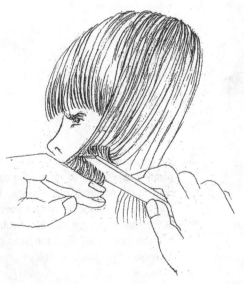

Take great care when using a razor. You must point the blade away from the knuckles. This creates a clubbed effect, not a tapered look.

The back

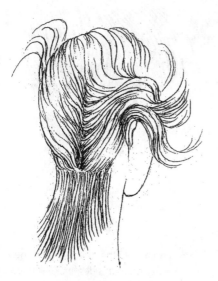

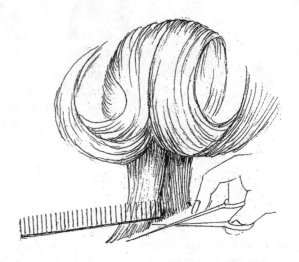

1. Before cutting the back section, part the hair down the centre back and swing the bulk of hair to either side. Wet hair usually holds back sufficiently, if well combed, to enable you to cut small sections at a time, but if the hair is thick and heavy use clips to anchor the excess bulk in place. You must cut a small section first as a guide, then bring down successive sections and cut them to match it.

2. When evening up the shape at the nape, use the comb pressed against the neck to control the ends. Then bring down successive sections from the bulk hair, and cut the rest of the back section, working to your guideline and keeping a check on the angle of your scissors. Do not force or stretch the hair: allow it to fall naturally. The nape should now be well shaped and slightly rounded.

3. It is very important to cut successive layers neatly and precisely so control the cut by holding the hair ends between your fingers. This hold is used mostly when creating a bevel at the ends on longer hair. But if you hold the hair too much away from the head and cut at an angle it will give a slight layering effect at the nape.

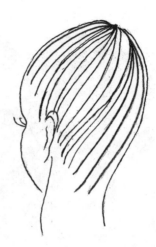

4. To even up the back and sides, the section immediately behind the ear should be lined up with the section in front of the ear and trimmed neatly and evenly. Leave the edge of the ear lobe exposed; do not try to conceal it.

Complete the cut by bringing down successive layers and cutting them to match the guideline. Follow the natural fall of the hair.

5. When cutting behind the ear in the basic cut always comb the hair to curve towards the line of the chin.

Errors and pitfalls to avoid

Many errors are made in this last part of the basic cut because of wrong directional combing. The correct rule in all basic cutting is *comb towards the chin*. This diagram shows the correct angle.

This hair has been combed incorrectly. In longer length hair the fault would not be noticeable because of the thickness of the hair, but on shorter lengths or styles where the bulk of the hair swings forward, the error will be plainly seen.

This uneven line is another fault produced as a result of incorrect combing.

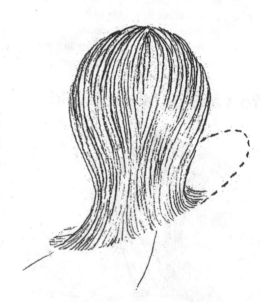

The first part of the cut is now complete. By using the basic cutting techniques this has created a frame around the head – the outer perimeter – based on the circle shape.

It is at this stage, before commencing the second part of the basic cut, that the bodying or micro-layering procedure should be carried out if it is required.

The bodying of hair

This is a special technique for cutting an invisible layering into the hair, a micro-layering in effect. It is not a thinning of hair (although, if necessary, bulk can be removed in this manner). It simplifies the dressing-out and manipulation of the hair when creating special effects. The hair is not shortened, in fact the mesh of hair must remain the same length. This technique is used by eminent stylists to achieve control over hair, particularly when preparing heads for special occasions such as display hairdressing and competition work. It should be used skilfully and invisibly to give the hair more body and control the final the dressing-out.

The illustrations show how the sections are lifted around the head using the razor to impart this body by lightly cutting under its own weight. Slip two or three strokes along the mesh, but never destroy the length and solidity of the hair. Continue section by section around the head, from the pivot-point of the crown, into the nape. With a little experience you will find this an invaluable and a more efficient addition to cutting than 'pointing' with the scissors. Pointing with the scissors is somewhat time-consuming and outdated and a little risky in unskilled hands. It was used by posticheurs (wig-makers) to take thickness away from around the wig where it fitted on to the forehead and face, to disguise a line or mark on the head or to take nape hair away. One of its uses some years ago was to cut the hair away crudely from the roots, in a series of partings throughout the hair, but when the hair grew a stubble showed. Eventually the slither cut with the scissors took its place as a much better way of reducing bulk. Pointing is a method which certain experienced hairdressers may feel is essential in order to create an effect and where time does not matter. The bodying technique illustrated here is practical and leaves you in full control of the cut. It is useful in everyday salon work and artistic fashion styling.

Bodying hair with a razor

1. This shows the direction of partings needed for the bodying procedure. The number of sections is not important provided they are all in the direction indicated.

3. The razor should be held at the angle shown here touching the hair under its own weight with no added pressure. Simply guide the razor which will take away a few hairs with each stroke along the mesh.

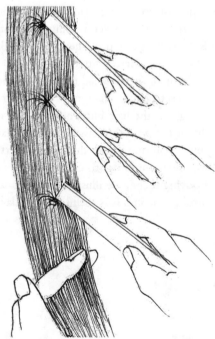

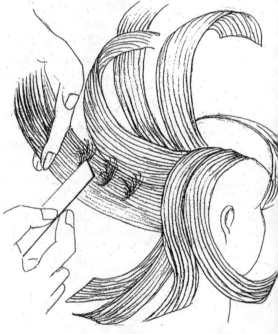

2. The bodying technique involves slipping the razor along the mesh of hair, with a few light, sliding strokes along the length, removing just a few hairs at a time, yet never destroying the solidity of the section.

4. Continue bodying the hair, section by section. Never allow the razor to cut right through and shorten the mesh of hair. This invisible micro-layering of the hair will simplify manipulation and gives maximum control with the brush during the dressing-out stage.

The basic cut: Stage Two

The second stage involves a layering process that needs an easy, methodical manner of working. Standing behind the head, comb all the hair back from the forehead. From now on use scissors only. The general pattern to be followed religiously in this part of the cut is to strike a parting from the centre forehead to the pivot point at the centre of the crown, and towards the centre of the nape. All further sections should be parallel to this centre guide. Do not deviate from this rule: never cut across the head.

Work at the front of the head first and, taking successive sections, cut backwards towards the crown. Do not cut the sides until the complete top and centre section of the head are completed. Study the illustrations of this part of the cut and note the disciplined manner of cutting, how each section is lifted up and held with the scissors parallel to the fingers and to the guideline. Always keep in mind that the head is a round shape. Note how the hair falls neatly into layers without distortion, like the leaves of an open book. The exact length must depend upon the texture, thickness and natural fall, and the final shape decided upon. In the style illustrated, the hair must be left slightly longer at the nape, therefore layering must stop at a point above the occipital bone. Should the intended style be based on a forward movement, then the layering procedure should be reversed and all cutting has to be done in a forward direction.

At the sides, which are longer and a little thicker, lift the hair in the same pattern parallel to the guidelines, not out from the head, but straight up. You will find that the correct length hair will fall away from the section held, leaving the excess lengths between the fingers to be cut off. Before finishing the layering, check and re-check, combing and lifting the hair, then combing towards the face from the crown, making sure there are no stray ends. Neatness and precision are important. Studying and practising this disciplined way of cutting will eventually establish a feeling of confidence and flair.

Layering

1. For the second stage the hair must be combed back, away from the forehead.

2. Now follow this precise plan for sectioning the hair. Take a parting from the centre forehead to the pivot point on the crown and then into the nape. All successive partings are parallel to this on the top of the head. For this style, a certain amount of layering is needed on the top of the head: the remainder of the hair is in longer lengths.

3. For a perfect layering technique the rules to follow are:
   a) All partings must made parallel to the mid-line of the scalp.
   b) The hair should be held straight up from the scalp, never angled away from it.
   c) The scissors must also cut parallel to the mid-line, never across the head.
   d) Start the layering at the front and then take successive sections of the hair backwards toward the crown and into the nape.

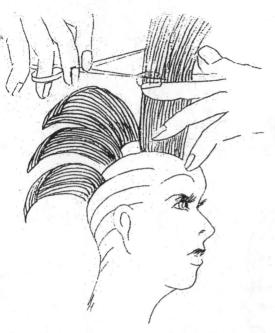

Do not simply cut mechanically, but feel the shape as you go. The layers must be cut to blend into the longer lengths at the back. This is an art which takes skill and practice.

This is the basic layer cut, the foundation of any hair style. Notice how the hair falls naturally into shape at the back of the head. Cutting this way will teach you to develop a real feel for hair so that, eventually, you will be able to produce any individual look or fashion.

Remember

Always hold the hair straight up to cut it and always cut parallel to the main parting from the centre forehead to the crown. Never cut across the head!.

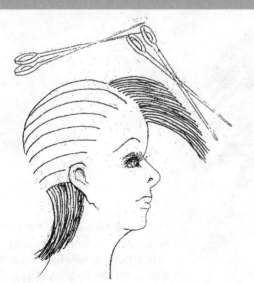

For a style based on a forward movement all the cutting must be done in the reverse manner, that is, in a forward direction.

This exaggerated view shows how the hair will fall if cut in a forward direction – just like the leaves of a book.

When cutting the sides, do not hold the hair out to the side, away from the head, or you may shorten some of the hair lengths. Always hold the hair straight up to cut it: the longer lengths will fall away automatically.

To finish off the basic cut, check and re-check the cut for any long stray strands that may have been left at the ends of the hair. Carefully and methodically lift and check each mesh as shown here. This is a very necessary part of the cut.

If the hair could be kept upright, the actual lengths across the top of the head on completion of the layered cut would look like this. If you want the side sections to be layered and graduated into the nape of the neck, merely carry the partings on the top of the head down to the ear and to the back of the head before cutting.

If you want the side lengths to be shorter continue the layering pattern down to the ear level and onto the back of the head. Always cut parallel to the centre guidelines; never across the head.

Cutting techniques and styles

There are many descriptions for the cut within the hairdressing vocabulary, such as Blunt Cut, Club Cut, Bevel Cut, Feather Cut, Razor Cut, Layer Cut, Scissor Cut, Thinning the hair, Taper cutting, Scissors-over-comb cutting etc. In addition there are terms that are descriptive of the mood in which the cut is presented, such as 'dimensional cutting' which means cutting to give length, breadth, to shorten, to lengthen; 'Geometric cutting' to give a geometric look, meaning square, blunt or bevel to the ends of the hair, and 'patterned cutting' to correspond to a particular mood and style.

Over the years there have been all kinds of looks and most eventually turn up again some years later with a slight variation and a different name. Whether it is the French look, the Italian cut, the Flapper of yesterday, or the Crop and Layer cut of today, it is hair cut with scissors or the razor, or even both, that achieves all.

There are only three ways hair can be cut:

a) Clubbed or Blunt cut.

b) Cut to a point (thinning or tapering).

c) A bevel on the end of the hair.

Remember

It is not what you cut off that counts, but what you leave behind!

These are described in more detail in the section on basic cuts in Chapter 3 (See page 20).

Do not be confused by the many different descriptions given to cutting. It is length that matters. Just keep to the rules and carry out your plan, using a methodical way of working. Your hands and fingers will sense the texture and length needed to cut a beautiful shape in the hair. Hair will always be changing length depending on the current mood or fashion. But cutting technique does not change, it is fashion and the moods of hairdressing that change. So learn to adapt your cut to any style with feeling and flare.

The basic one-length cut

When cutting a one-length cut, it is important to note the shape, texture and the way the hair weight is distributed throughout the head. It is also necessary to establish, in the very beginning, what shape you want to create at the points. You could achieve a curved look or one of a variety of straight falls around the face. Use the 'circle guideline' to help you as you comb the hair and note the natural fall, direction of growth and condition of the hairline, as all these could affect the final shape.

Having decided on the length and what shape you want at the ends, part the hair down the centre of the head at the back and cut a small section of hair as a guideline at the nape. Cut the first section on the neckline, then bring down the remainder of the hair in convenient sections until the bulk of the hair is ready to be given a final edging and bevelling. Check the cutting blades of the scissors are evenly placed when bevelling the final lengths. Be careful at the sides of the head when finishing off the cut. Comb and re-comb, making sure there are no distortions, or an awkward pull at the roots which could change the shape at the points and check and re-check the fall of the hair while bevelling the last cutting on the ends of the hair.

The basic one-length cut

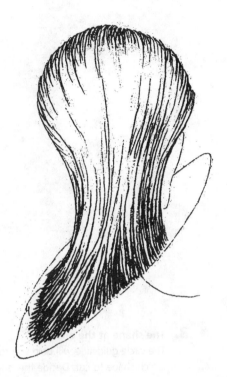

1. The hair should be wet, having been shampooed and combed through, freeing the hair of tangles. Comb the hair and carefully note its natural fall. Take note of the condition of the hairline, especially the direction of growth. The aim is to cut an outline – a circle shape – around the ends of the hair.

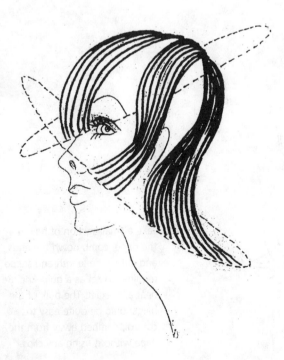

2. Always imagine a circle as a guideline. Circles dictate the fall of the fringe in the top section and the natural downwards direction for the remainder of the shape. This creates a lovely natural balance between shape and line.

3. **The shape at the ends:**
   The circle guideline will help you to decide which shape to cut. Decide the length, direction of the loop or curve and shape at the ends.

4. Take a small section of hair in the nape, comb down the ends and cut to the length and shape required to act as a guideline. Be neat and exact. The bulk of the hair should be quite easy to control, combed away from the nape without using any clips.

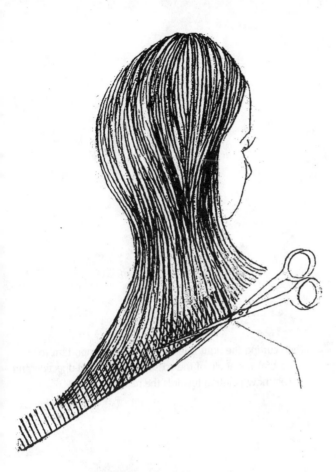

5. The remainder of the hair can now be cut in convenient sections until the bulk of the hair is ready to be given a final edging. Keep the hair flat to the head. Use the comb as shown to control the ends. Check the shape falls cleanly and neatly at the nape. The blade of the scissors should hang down slightly towards the shoulder.

6. Be sure the hair fall is correct and natural when finalizing the cutting of the sides. Comb and re-comb, making certain there are no distortions and wayward pulls at the roots that could change the shape at the ends.

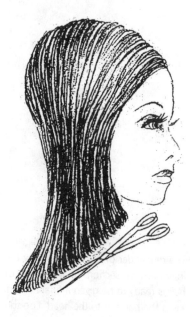

7. When cutting the right side of the head it is important to realize that the angle of the scissors has changed direction and they are now pointing towards the nape.

Slight overlap on the last cut

Scissors angle on final cut

8. On the left side use the corner of the mouth and the distance from the lobe of the ear as a guideline. Complete the cut by checking the edges all round the perimeter. There should be a slight overlap on the last layer cut to enable the ends to turn under.

'Setting' was originally known as the *'mis-en-plis'* which is French for 'put-in-place'. This became abbreviated to just 'the pli' or 'setting'. It is still known internationally known as the *mis-en-plis*.

First of all, you should understand the simple theory behind the setting patterns applied where the hair is moulded and positioned while it is wet. You must learn to use the setting tools and equipment correctly, especially the comb and tail-comb which are used for moulding the wet hair, and you must discipline your hands and fingers so that eventually they will instinctively obey your thinking. Moulding the wet hair before putting in curl pins and rollers is very important if the final stage, the 'dressing-out', is to be carried out successfully.

Rollers

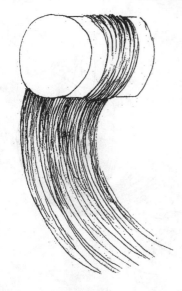

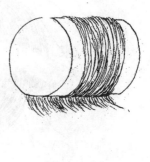

1. Take a section of the hair, lift the mesh upwards as you comb the ends smooth. Place the ends of the hair evenly around the roller before turning the roller downwards towards the curve at the root. Avoid excessive pulling or this will distort the shape you have created by combing.

2. As the roller turns, take care that the root does not drag. This is a very common error mainly caused by careless winding. Never disturb the roots once the roller is fixed in place.

3. Fit the roller snugly into the curve of the root. The mesh of hair should follow one curved shape flowing from the roots to the points. Rollers are an easy way of holding a movement firmly in place.

Good rollering

The two rollers show how the root movements blend together perfectly. It is important to put in rollers neatly and precisely.

Bad rollering

A carelessly placed roller may conceal the root and prevents you from noticing that there is drag at the root.

Pin-curls

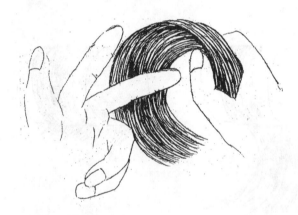

Stand-up pin-curl or barrel curl

1. Take a section of wet hair and comb the root hair upwards, pressing the middle finger of the left hand into the curve as the right thumb and forefinger take control of the ends. As you pull the hair towards you, exert a little pressure. The middle finger of the left hand, countering the pull of the right hand, has forced a curve at the roots.

2. Next, close the forefinger of the left hand towards the middle finger to take control of the mesh of hair. With the right hand, use the tail comb to turn the ends in, making sure that they are smooth and aligned with the curve at the root.

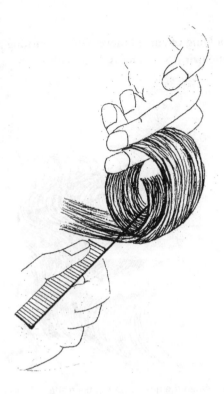

3. With the tail comb, firmly turn the ends tight into the curve, while at the same time pushing down towards the scalp. The left hand should counter this with a pull upwards, still controlling the mesh of hair. Keep the tail comb firmly in position while you withdraw the middle finger, leaving the curl upright ready to be secured with the clip.

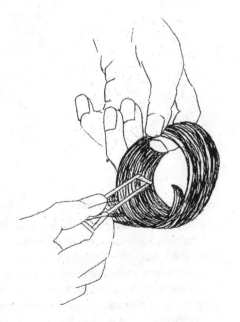

4. Hold the curl with your forefinger and thumb while you put the clip in place to hold the ends into the root curve. The clip should be opened first before sliding the bottom half into position, and then closing it. Do not push the clip fully into the curl: only the end of the clip should grip.

Moulding the hair

A vital part of pin-curling is the moulding of curved movement by creating a waved shape with the comb while the hair is wet. This is done with just a comb and the fingers.

Finger waving

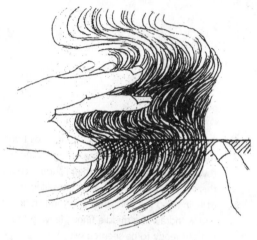

1. Having created the first wave with the comb, place the middle finger of the left hand over it. At the same time, use the comb in the right hand to stroke the hair in the opposite direction to form a crest.

2. When the next wave has been shaped, place the index finger of the left hand just underneath the crest of the waved shape.

Joining up wave movements

Enlarge the wave movements one at a time. Start by controlling adjoining hair with the middle finger and comb. The technique is virtually the same as creating a wave, but several combing strokes are necessary to blend the edges together, using the tip of the middle finger and the tip of the comb, to join one wave to the next.

The classic wave

1. To blend the edges of the waves together, start by merging the first wave from the lower side of the parting into the second wave of the other side, on the crown of the head.

2. The third wave from the higher side of the parting merges into the second wave on the lower side. While sculpting the first and second waves on the crown, take care to just gently etch the shape of the wave.

1. (left) Do not force the movements on the crown where the waves merge. Merely shadow the natural shape by gently stroking and etching the wave shapes with the comb and tip of the middle finger. Only begin to intensify the depth of the wave at the third and fourth wave movements.

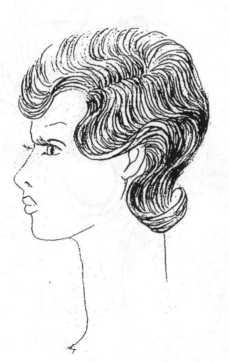

2. (above) As the peaks of the waves are sculpted towards the face, avoid pinching the crests or disturbing the roots by pushing. You can deepen the crests by using a series of stroking movements using the comb and fingertip.

3. (left) Space the wave movements evenly throughout the head, balancing the width on each side. The widest wave should be just underneath the occipital bone, at the back of the head.

Pin-curling

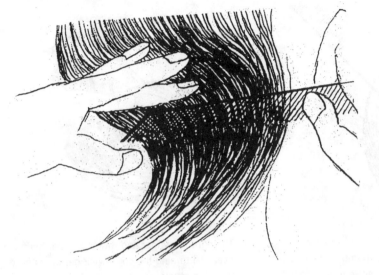

1. In preparation for making a clockwise pin-curl, mould the hair using your middle finger to steady the circular movement created from the roots with the comb.

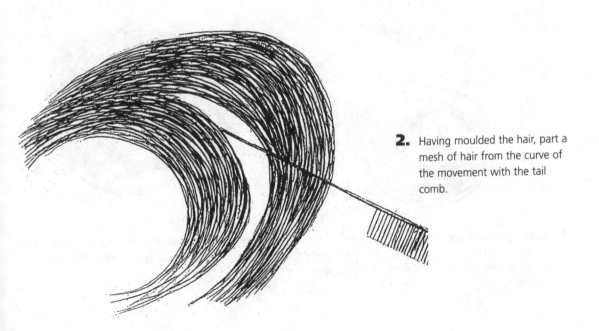

2. Having moulded the hair, part a mesh of hair from the curve of the movement with the tail comb.

A clockwise curl

1. Use the tail of a comb to control the curve of the mesh of hair as the forefinger and thumb of your left hand hair guide the tips into a circle to lie against the roots.

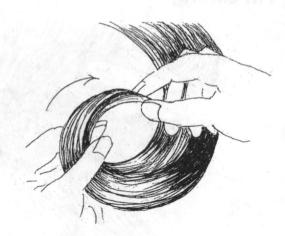

2. The right forefinger and thumb should then take over, still turning the coil of hair gently, without disturbing the root yet keeping firm control of the ends.

3. Work from above the mesh of hair and not underneath. The curl is completed as the ends are eased into the curve beside the root. No forcing is necessary.

4. Hold the curl with the left hand and use the tail comb to tidy any stray ends into the curve.

5. Use the tail comb as a lever to ease the hair tips firmly against the bend of the curl before it is clipped to the roots.

6. Open the clip and slide the bottom half into the curve first, before closing the clip to secure the curl at the points, leaving the other side free.

An anti-clockwise curl

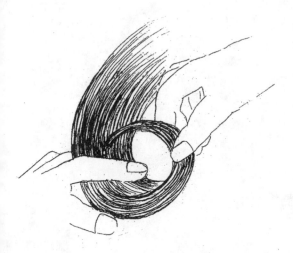

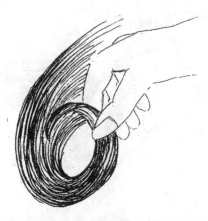

1. Use the tail comb to separate off a mesh of hair. Use the forefinger of your left hand to control the inner curve of the mesh. Let the thumb and forefinger of your right hand take control of the hair tips and turn them into a curve. Always work from above the curl. Never allow the fingers to stray and work their way underneath the curl as this will distort the final shape.

2. Hold the curl in position with your thumb and forefinger, ready for the left hand to take over and guide the points into the finished curl.

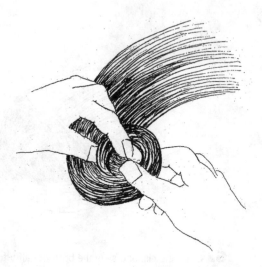

3. Working from above, use your thumb and forefinger of the left hand to lay the points of the curl into the curve at the root. Do not twist or tighten the coil of hair. A good curl is a beautifully controlled circle from root to points.

4. Slide your thumb and forefinger gently together while still holding the hair tips. This will enable them to settle easily into the bend of the curl and will help the clip to secure the curl more easily to the root.

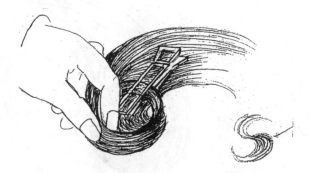

5. Secure the curl with the clip to the root leaving one side of the completed curl free. One side of a pin-curl should always be left free, otherwise the resulting shape will be squared and the crest of the wave that is formed will be distorted.

Planning the setting pattern

In every set there are three areas to consider – the top, sides and back. Nature itself indicates where these areas lie. The receding point of the hairline at the temple on either side of the forehead is the start of the circle guideline for the set on the top of the head. This is the key to the setting technique. Follow the diagrams for the setting plans methodically. You will see that they all follow logical rules.

Learning to model the wet hair with the comb is very important in setting. You must learn to control root movement with your comb and then not to disturb the shape when placing a roller or a pin-curl. In addition, some current styles often need no rollering but are modelled and moulded with the fingers and comb, using a special gel or setting lotion, to give a subtle waved shape, with fluffy, delicate tendrils stroked in at the forehead and sides before leaving to set.

Blow-drying

When blow-drying you must understand the principles of root control as these affect the shape and movement of hair wet. Would-be hairdressers struggle with blow-drying hair because they know nothing about root control.

Pin-curling

It is important to establish good habits when pin-curling. Your fingers must never stray underneath the mesh when curling the hair tips inwards, but should always stay on the outside. This is the correct way to pin-curl. If your fingers get underneath the hair they may get in the way and cause you to twist the root.

Take care with the clip. Never clip across the curl, simply secure the points to the root leaving the rest of the curl free.

The perfect set

Remember

Work from above the mesh of hair, never underneath.

Following a strict routine is important in every stage of hairdressing, but particularly in setting. You must keep to your plan or pattern of working, concentrating on controlling the root hair and movements first and foremost as this is the key to correct setting. Stroke and comb and comb again before making a movement – a curl – or placing a roller. Perfect setting will result in good line, shape and movement which create the basis for the final dressing-out. It will be easy to add the finishing touches if a good foundation has been created.

The natural fall of the hair when wet indicates the partings and direction in which rollers or pin-curls should be wound. This illustration shows an example of growth-direction at the front of the forehead with the dominant fall of the hairline to one side. These are very important points to consider when planning the hair style.

In this example of directional setting the natural direction of growth on the forehead gives a forward movement. The hair has been sectioned with the partings following the natural lie of the hair. By winding the hair onto rollers in this way, the set will not show partings at the root when it is brushed out.

The setting pattern here follows the same rule as for cutting: the receding point at the temples has been used to start a parting which forms a circle around the back of the crown. The comb held at the back of the head as shown indicates the void that must be filled and shows where to finish the setting of the top of the head. Notice how the first parting follows the slope of the hairline.

The circle method applied to setting

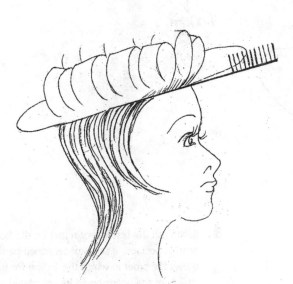

The *circle method* is an organized way of placing rollers on the top, sides and back of the head. This is one of the basic principles of setting and is the foundation for the various lines, shapes and styles described later. The basic setting pattern should be neat and precise. Always comb each mesh of hair to control the roots before putting in a roller.

Use the tail comb to follow the natural line of the hairline on the brow as a guide to positioning the first line of rollers. The 'circle' guideline defines the crown area.

The crown

1. (left) Start the setting on the forehead, using the two receding points of the hairline on either side of the temple as a guideline. Place the first line of rollers on the right side, starting at the parting which should be immediately off-centre to the left. The eyebrow can be used as a guide for positioning the off-centre parting.

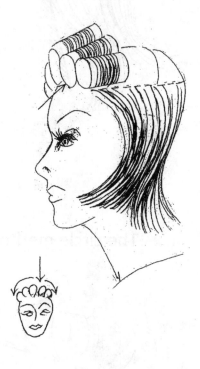

2. (right) Now turn to the left side and place two more rollers parallel with the others.

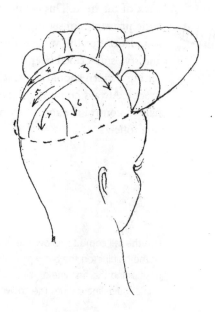

3. (left) With the first line of rollers on the front of the head in position, a series of sectioned partings shows the order in which the setting for the top, or crown, of the head should be completed. Notice how they alternate from side to side. This is also the basis for various other styles.

4. Make another parting on the right side of the head and place the next set of rollers. All the partings must be neat and accurate.

5. Now put in the rollers on the left side to complete the second row.

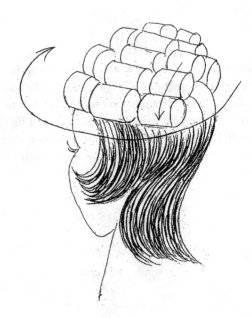

6. The third row of rollers shows the plan for the crown beginning to take shape. Three rollers are directed towards the back of the head to start filling in the gap at the back.

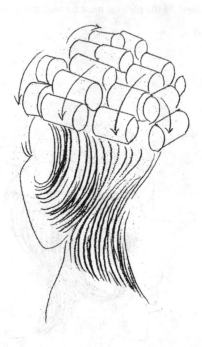

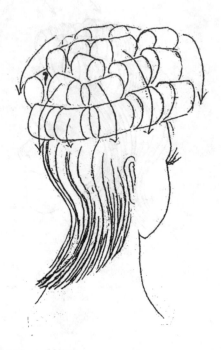

7.   Next, two rollers are directed backwards leaving a
gap for the last, single roller to complete the
crown. The shape of the head has been followed
to achieve a balanced look. A well-planned setting
pattern like this will produce a good final result.

The crown complete

The 'top of the head' circle, or crown, is now complete
with the last single roller in place, facing backwards.

The sides

<table>
<tr><td>

Remember

The curl must curve
from the root to the
point.

</td><td>

Before even attempting to roller any kind of shape you should mould the
hair at the sides into a curve. Remember the basic rule: stroke and comb the
curve before making any curl or movement in order to control the
movement from the root to the hair tips. This shape must not be disturbed
when it is put into a roller or pin-curl. Some of the most common faults are
made at this stage, due to careless winding which is unseen until the dressing-
out, which is too late.

</td></tr>
</table>

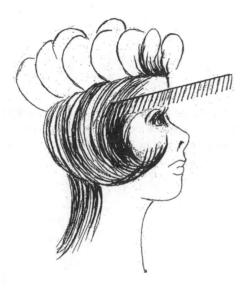

1. Mould the hair into a curve with the comb. The middle finger of the left hand can be used to steady the centre of the curve as the comb passes through the hair, exactly as you would when creating a waved shape.

2. With the point of the tail comb, part a section of the hair into a curve. Do not disturb or distort this shape when winding this onto a roller (or making it into a pin-curl).

The nape

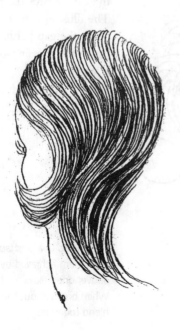

Another place to look for any natural lie of the hair is at the back of the head, just underneath the occipital bone, at the nape. The hair there usually has a dominant swing either to the right or the left. Check this point before finalizing the setting at the nape, especially with shorter hair. Both rollers and pin-curls are shown for setting the nape as the same rules apply to both. Rollers are more common, but the pin-curl technique is useful to know, especially for short hair.

The hair at the nape usually has a dominant swing either to the right or left. Moulding the hair with the comb into the dip just underneath the bone will show a very pronounced swing to one side of the nape or the other. This is the largest wave movement and all rollering must follow the swing of this movement.

(left) At one side of the nape, where the bend of the hair meets the opposite movement behind the ear, both movements must be blended together, using the reverse curl technique.

The reverse curl or 'one above, one below' rule

The curl or roller behind the ear is fixed in the opposite direction to the one above which curves towards the face. This rule can be applied wherever a blend of movement is needed with one curl in one direction and one in the opposite, creating an 'S' shape as shown here. There is often a temptation to place a curl or roller behind the ear towards the face. The illusion is that it will cover the gap behind the ear in the dressing-out, but it will not!

One above, one below:

The roller behind the ear should curve towards the nape, the one above curves towards the face.

This shows the 'S' shaped movement achieved by the 'one above, one below' method. When brushed out the curls will blend together.

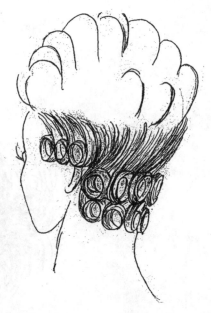

The rollers must be fixed neatly into the movement at the nape with the 'one above, one below rule' applied where the back curls meet the sides.

The nape can also be set in pin-curls. The same rules apply: both curls and rollers must be neatly positioned following the natural movement of the hair and , once again, the 'one above, one below rule' is applied where the nape meets the sides.

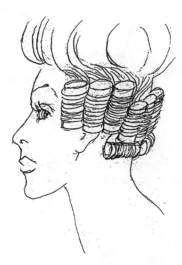

At the sides, the rollers should be fixed parallel with the hair curving towards the face. Mould each mesh of hair carefully before wrapping it on the roller, and never twist the hair at the root.

Pin-curls can also be used for setting at the sides. The curls must be positioned carefully with the root movement undisturbed. These curls have been placed so that, on dressing- out, this movement can have a 'dual' effect: either a soft wave hugging the face, or the hair flicked towards the face, depending on the length of the hair.

The finished look

This is the result of the 'one above and one below rule', though effects may vary from head to head depending upon texture and length of hair.

Adapting the basic set

The following illustrations show various setting plans and the styles achieved in dressing- out. Notice the change of direction of the roller placing within the top circle shape for the top of the head.

Depending on the length of the hair, with a basic set variations in style can be created in the dressing-out stage.

The top of the head

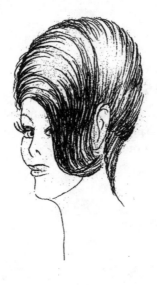

For this style all the rollers within the circle shape are directed to one side. The dressing- out follows the movement created.

In this style three rollers in the top circle are directed towards the front. When dressed-out this creates a very pretty fringed look which suits high foreheads.

Here, the roller plan for the top of the head includes a central line of rollers directed backwards. This results in a symmetrical fall of hair on either side of the forehead.

The back

This shape will suit a tall person with a long neck. The back rollers are fixed in the occipital area and are directed forward. A few small barrel curls or rollers at the front create a delicate fringe to offset height.

For a shape that creates a dramatic effect, the top of the head and the back can be moulded into one simple movement with the hair sides flicked up at the sides with the help of a hot brush or a few rollers below the ear.

This is the standard setting plan for creating a turned-under or classic page-boy look with longer hair.

nine  The dressing-out

This is where the ability of the craftsman shows. The final dressing-out depends on how well the cutting has been done, but there is more praise to be won by learning dressing-out techniques correctly.

The dressing-out technique used depends upon what kind of result is required. Setting, blow-drying and all kinds of curling effects may be involved but in classical hairdressing there is a basic dressing-out procedure and this can be adapted to suit different styles. Today's casual hairstyles are deceptive – the very simple look relies on a knowledge of controlled dressing-out.

The brush is an essential tool - one to choose carefully. A firm, well-made brush of artificial fibre is usually the best choice, as this goes through the hair to the roots and blends the movements smoothly without causing any damage to the hair. The client will be aware of the care and craftsmanship that has gone into the cut and set, but it is the brushing that creates that final impression of beautiful shape and line. Different brushing methods are needed for certain types of hair and cutting styles. You brush to obtain line, shape and movement – not just to loosen rollered hair! Good brushing should result in control of snarling and snagging and elimination of tight curl and roller separations. From this will follow the distribution of hair to obtain the movement, shape and lovely outline.

The principal function of the brush is to reduce tension in the curl or waved movement created by the use of rollers, pin-curls, hot brush, irons, etc.

Each brush stroke is usually used in conjunction with the comb in order to achieve a smooth continuous flow with the brush. If the stroking action cannot be completed in one movement successive strokes may be needed as the comb and brush encounter some snagging. Stop and start again, using the comb to precede the brush to free the movement. Practise this technique if you want to achieve a smooth conditioned, textured look, with shape and line without any back-brushing or back-combing.

Sometimes two brushes are used but, unless you are ambidextrous, this is not advisable. It is rare for both hands to be able to control equally well, so the curl will be loosened without acquiring shape.

Basic brushing movements

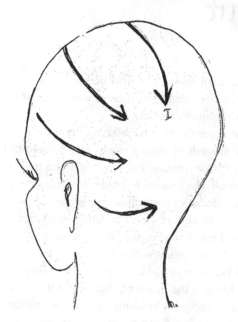
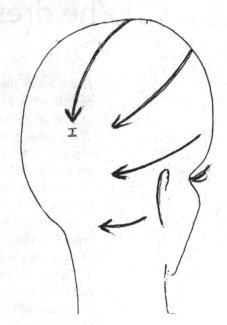

There are four indispensable brush strokes. The first action should start at the centre forehead and go through to the centre nape. The procedure is exactly the same on both sides of the head.

The brush

Hold the brush firmly using the thumb and forefinger to give you good control.

Use the thumb behind the brush when using hard stokes to brush across the back of the head.

The brush is an essential tool and must be carefully chosen. It must be a firm and the bristles must penetrate to the scalp without scratching it. As it glides through the bulk it should texture the hair. It must be a proper dressing-out brush, not one of the plastic or wire brushes that are used in blow drying, or to disentangle matted hair; they merely loosen hair but do not control movement.

Every brush stroke should be used in conjunction with a comb stroke preceding it. The comb smooths the way for the brush

Take two or three strokes along the length of the hair right through to the ends.

Never start to dress the hair at the root. Brush through the points first, then the middle lengths to remove any tangles before brushing right through the length from the roots to the points. The final brush strokes must always begin at the forehead and finish at the nape, or be taken from one side of the head to the other. Bind or backcomb the complete shape and flick the dressing-out comb over the points to control unruly ends.

Work always from above, never underneath, and aim to achieve a particular shape. It is important to acquire this 'feel' for hair shape. A well-executed dressing-out may be technically perfect but this does not guarantee its beauty – there are other considerations that matter. There must be design-shape-direction of movement in a hair style, and the line should not be rigid – it must flow and have balance. It must reveal your client's best attributes. Just as light discloses the many facets of a diamond, so should the line and dressing of a hair style reveal the many sides of a person's personality and looks.

There are four indispensable brushing strokes which should be studied and practised. Practise just holding and rolling a brush in your hand, letting the thumb and forefinger change alternately. Note how the brush becomes an extension to your hand and forearm in action. Keep brushing until you can complete the movement without encountering snagging.

In the softer fashion styling, the brush alone should be sufficient to dress hair. The hair must be smooth and untangled. Back-combing is unnecessary and should only be used discreetly when a style demands a certain holding power. Even then, a 'binding procedure' may take its place. This is a 'fluffing' action with the comb, similar to back-brushing, where the comb is pushed forwards at intervals along a mesh without destroying the movement of a shape or line. The movement is then bound with the brush, giving a lovely natural look.

Left side

1. Brush from the centre forehead to the centre nape. Learn to feel what is happening with each stroke. If the brush catches a knot or snarl, stop and start again at that spot, continuing the stroke until you can complete the movement without encountering a snag. Some hairdressers use a comb to help disentangle the hair, others use only a brush.

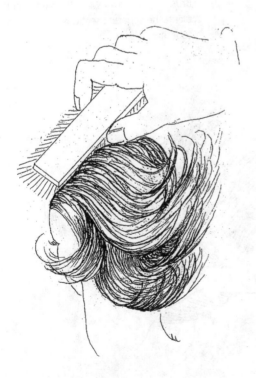

2. Brush from above the temple across the back to the side of the nape on the right. This should reduce tension in the curl or wave movement.

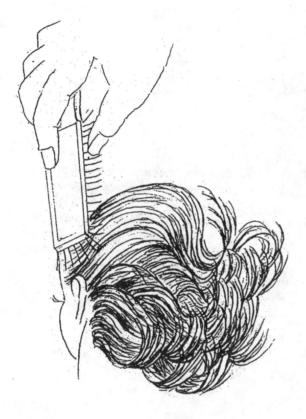

When brushing above the ear and the back of the head where the tension in the wave movement may be stronger, it is important to feel the elasticity and spring in the hair relaxing. It is only ready to be finished off when it is feels controlled and a single stroke of the brush shows that the movement is well textured and there is no kick-back from the curl.

3. Start from above the left ear, taking all the hair across the back of the head to the other side. The forefinger guides until the thumb takes over as the brush glides towards the nape. Brushing in this way will reduce the curl and blend the separate sections of the setting together.

4. Brush from behind the ear at the nape across the back of the head to the other side. The bottom end of the brush, nearest the forefinger, starts the stroke in this part of the brushing. The thumb takes over at the back of the head. This brushing helps to control excessive tightness and snarl, especially at the nape.

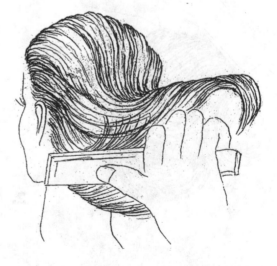

Right side

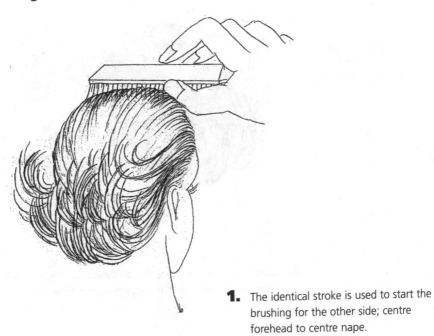

1. The identical stroke is used to start the brushing for the other side; centre forehead to centre nape.

2. Brush from the right temple, across the head to the nape on the left side. The brush should be directed with a sloping action to the left.

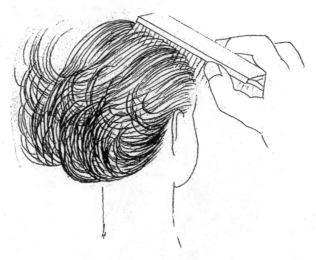

3. Start just above the ear, taking in the hair across the back. The brush strokes are identical on each side but in opposite directions.

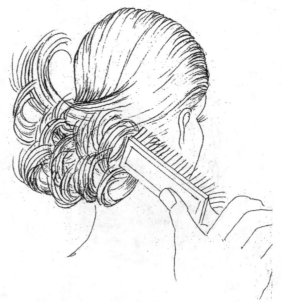

4. Blend the nape hair across the back of the head towards the opposite side. Direct the brush towards the other ear using the thumb to glide the brush across the nape.

5. The follow-on after the comb
Every stroke used so far must be used in conjunction with the comb. This is to achieve a smooth continuous flow of the brush. As each stroke cannot be completed in one movement, successive strokes are needed as the comb and brush encounter some snarling and snagging. Stop and start again, using the comb to precede the brush to free the movement.

6. Make two or three strokes along the length of the hair right through to the ends. These are necessary to control the hair and blend the movements into shape. You brush to obtain a line – shape and movement – not just to loosen hair that has

Binding or fluffing technique

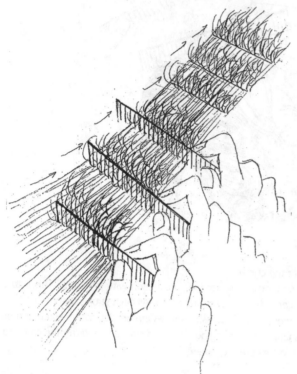

To bind the hair, hold a section of hair firmly between the forefinger and middle finger with your thumb pressing down on the forefinger to give added strength. Make a progressive series of strokes upwards along the length of the mesh of hair, pushing a few hairs forward each time, but never reaching the stroke before. This fluffing action binds the hair together. Always work from the top of the mesh, never underneath, and do not push the comb into the roots. Use the broad-toothed part of the comb.

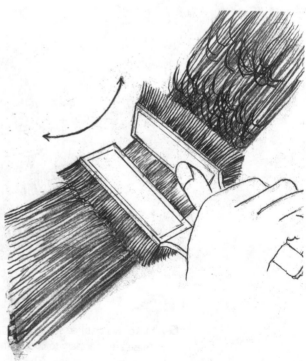

This binding action can also be achieved in the same way using a brush with a swinging wrist action.

1. (left) Always start binding at the front of the head. The brush should already have created the outline of the style and all the comb does it to emphasize the shape, adding volume and height where necessary. As with cutting and setting, the hairline and the area between the temples provide a natural key to the shape.

2. (above) Work around the front and then the top of the head. The style will gradually take shape naturally. Do not attempt to dress-out or finish the hair at this point, just create volume, as shown in the picture inset.

3. (left) Do not separate the hair into sections, simply pick up a mesh at random and fluff it up with the comb to bind it. Always work from above. Remember not to push the comb into the roots, as in back-combing, as this is extremely difficult to brush out. Binding is kinder to the hair.

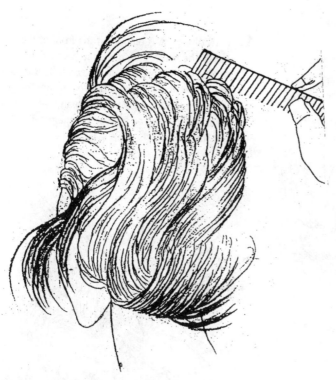

1. To finalize the dressing-out, after binding the top area of hair just flick the ends gently into place - do not comb the roots as this will flatten the hair again.

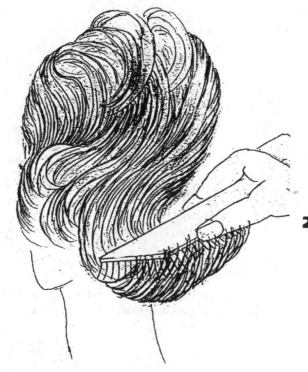

2. To control the back movement, place the brush at the curve at the back of the head, just under the occipital bone, gripping the brush firmly with thumb and forefinger. Dig the brush in slightly and pull the curl movement gently upwards and outwards to allow the movement to fall into place.

3. To control the side movements, hold the curved ends firmly between your fingers and fluff up the mesh with a few strokes of the comb pushed gently into the curve, then just leave it. Do not comb it out.

4. With long hair, this binding technique can also used on the bulk of the hair which must be gripped firmly while the fluffing procedure is done. Once again, you must always work from above.

Lacquer

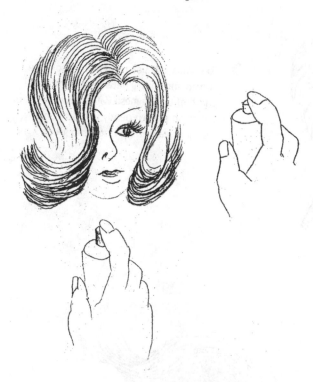

Dressing-out can be finished off by spraying it with lacquer. The spray should be held at least nine inches away from the head and be directed away from the face towards the back of the head to avoid spray getting in the eyes or on the face.

Lacquer should be used with discretion, working around the head and spraying in short bursts rather than one continuous spray.

PART THREE

Styling

ten Face shapes

The right hairstyle can flatter the face. It can emphasize the perfect shape, or it can minimize all the defects giving an illusion of perfection. Study the bone structure of the head and face in order to decide on the most suitable style. When dealing with long and short necks, high foreheads, twisted and distorted hairlines, etc. it may be necessary to disguise these features. For instance, a long neck may be lovely to look at but, if it is really too long in relation to a person's height, it requires a flattering hairstyle to balance it. In a case such as this, very short hair or hair swept on top of the head, should be avoided. Styles taken to the top of the head and away from the forehead will make a short neck look slimmer and longer.

Foreheads often need masking with a fringe shape, either to cover an excessively high hairline or to disguise a distorted hairline. Fringes play a very important part in hairstyling. They can be used most effectively to distract attention from heavily-boned and square facial features, a receding chin and high forehead. Alternatively, a fringe can draw attention to a perfect bone structure and emphasize the eyes most dramatically. Tiny fringes can soften a severe-looking style as well as add an impish look to a short and bubbly hairstyle.

Study the contours of the head. Where the proportions are too narrow or too small, the hair is used to fill out the contours in the bone structure around the face. Similarly, keep the hair close and tailored to the head where the bone structure of the face is too broad, round or square. Remember also the back of the head, and notice not only the length of the neck but the person's height, the width of the physique, the breadth and roundness of the shoulders. All of these points will have a bearing on the length and shape of the hairstyle at the neckline.

Notice where the widest point is across the brow, the cheekbones or jaw, then decide which of the basic face shapes a style will suit.

The basic face shapes

1. The oval

The oval is the perfect shape, simply because its overall width and length are ideal. Any kind of styling, long or short, blends beautifully with the perfect bone structure and is immediately flattering.

An oval face shape can create a bold sophisticated hair style, or it can be a simple baby-doll look. The hair can be parted at the side, centre, or swept away boldly from the forehead. Really, provided the defects are nil, virtually any shape will show off the face to perfection.

2. The long square

The long square, or oblong, can be treated in various ways but basically the object is to reduce the apparent length. This is done very simply by curving a fringe downwards, with the length at the sides rounding to about jaw length, thus creating an oval shape.

The oblong or long square has forehead, cheekbones and jawline of almost equal width. Choose a style that adds softness and adds width to minimize length. Hair should be taken on to the face rather than away from it.

3. The round and the square

The round and the square have exceptional width at the cheeks, although the round tapers slightly at the temples. Many of the techniques for dealing with the round shape also apply to the square. To create an oval, tailor the sides and add height. Often a slightly asymmetrical tilt will help offset the severity of the square and round if the style is balanced correctly.

A round hairline, low forehead and rounded cheeks are the usual characteristics of a round face. With these drawbacks, partings will be difficult to place. Ideally, an asymmetrical effect similar to that applied to the square face is best. A slight fringe, covering a corner of the forehead, will soften the overall effect. You should create an oval by adding height and keeping width away from the sides.

A square face usually has the chin and jawline almost as wide as the forehead. Therefore a style must be chosen to emphasize length. Geometric cuts, straight lines and anything that adds width should be avoided. If the hair is long, tailor the shape away from the face and below the ears at the back of the head. A slight asymmetrical tilt at the front will soften the overall shape.

4. The inverted triangle

The inverted triangle has very wide cheekbones and width at the temple with a narrowing at the chin. It is often described as 'heart-shaped'. Variations on a medium length bob or flick-ups with a delicate fringed shape can give as near an illusion of the oval as is possible.

The inverted triangle is usually a pretty face shape, sometimes known as 'heart-shaped'. Medium length hair with a bob shape is ideal as it fills the gap at jaw level. Another good shape is the flick-up look as it balances the narrowing of the face shape beautifully.

5. The triangle

The triangle is the opposite of heart-shaped and is referred to as being 'pear-shaped', since the area around jaw level is the widest. This needs a clinging shape to slim the face, while at the forehead the hair should be layered short enough to be swept across the hairline to increase the illusion of width at the temples.

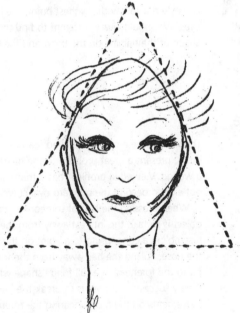

The triangle has a wide jawline in combination with a narrow forehead and is often referred to as being 'pear-shaped'. This needs a clinging shape to slim the face. Choose a short and layered shape with the hair swept across the forehead to emphasize and give width at the temples. Avoid longer hair with any fluffiness around the ears as this will widen and emphasize the lower part of the face.

The features

Eyes

The eyes and the eyebrows must be considered together in deciding the line of a hairstyle, especially within the temple area. The eyes and mouth are the most changeable and expressive of the facial features.

Seen sideways on, the eyebrows take one of three definite lines. It may be seen as totally horizontal, rising or on a downward line. Should a hairstyle not follow the highest point, the hair will tend to hang in the eyes. We should always attempt to find the right balance between the shape of the hairline on the brow and the line of the eyes.

Nose

The nose is the most outstanding feature of the face and one that can, at times, present a great problem to the hairdresser. The nose is shaped like a wedge. Viewed in profile it has a triangular form which normally does not extend beyond the outward oval curve of the face.

When dressing the hair of someone with a very prominent nose, the object is to take the interest away from the nose. Therefore anything resembling a cone, rising to a point on the crown, will only accentuate the nose. Pulling the hair away from the forehead or throwing the hair on to the forehead in a full fringe shape will also create the wrong effect. A very successful answer is to break the hairline into two curved movements on the brow, clearing the forehead over one eye and sweeping low over the other. These two curved movements focus the interest on the eyes and forehead taking attention away from the nose.

Mouth

Because modern make-up tends to over-emphasize the mouth, the importance of the lips can present the hairstylist with some difficulties. Cosmetic fashions are forever changing the line and shape of the mouth so that it can be difficult to harmonize shorter hair shapes with them. If the mouth has an unfortunate line, avoid hair shapes that hang at lip level and draw attention to it.

Ears

The average size for an ear is one quarter the length of the head or the length of the nose. Its top should align with the eyebrow and the bottom be on line with the nostril. Ideally the ear should not stand off the head more than the space of its own thickness. Most outward lines on the head point towards the ear. The line of the hair at the temple, the curve at the throat, and the line at the jaw, point towards the ear.

However unattractive an ear is, to cover it entirely can produce an even worse effect. The top of the ear can be disguised by slightly arranging the hair to mask its shape and position.

Neck lines

It is important to consider the neck line of a hairstyle when planning a style.
You may have to contend with problems of growth distortions at the root
hair, excessive curl or harsh, straight, spiky roots, some of which can be
disguised by tailoring the shape of the hair at the nape. The face profile
should act as a guide as to whether to cut the hair long or short. Longer hair
tends to soften and fill in spaces, while shorter hair leaves a stark bareness.
Neck lines, too, can be long, short, full, narrow and wide, and neck length
will usually determine the way the hair is cut at the nape to balance a line or
design.

The basic styling rules can be applied as a guide to cutting hair at the nape.
Tall people need longer hair at the nape, since the neck is long; a plump
person may have a short neck that needs lengthening and narrowing; a
shorter person will need a long look above the shoulders and at the nape; a
thin neck needs a full shape which will soften and flatter the neck line.

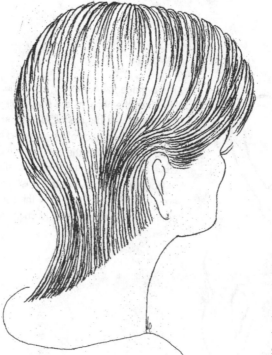

In this cut at the nape
on a short neck the hair
has been angled towards
the middle, which
lengthens the back of
the head at the nape,
though the ends remain
softly natural on the
hairline.

This neckline cut can be used to offset a distinctly unruly hairline where the growth is vigorous. The shape lends itself to controlling wiry hair where the shape at the nape needs to be a little thicker and heavier, with no excess layering, in order to lose the spikiness and the resistant pull of strong root movement.

This shape serves well for a long neck where the hairline either side and behind the ears grows defiantly downwards and refuses to be controlled in other ways. It is easier to use this downward shape and square it low down on the neck in order to soften and shorten a long look. The awkward growths behind the ears are left as natural as possible, layering just enough to control thickness. The points are edged carefully to give a neat, tailored look.

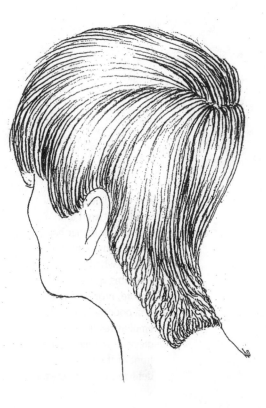

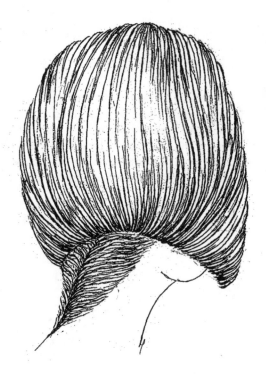

To lengthen a short neck which has an excessively thick growth at the nape, the hair can be deliberately cut across the back, level with the jawline, in a short, bevelled fashion. The hair underneath is layered and shaped neatly, finishing it off with a triangular movement into the centre to add an illusion of length.

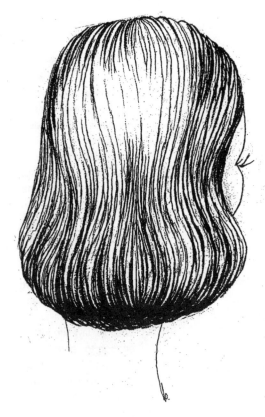

This neck line is natural and uncluttered and suitable for longer hair. The length is ideal for anyone who has problems with hair texture, protruding ears, or a poor hairline as it emphasizes the long drape of the hair at the front of the head. It is definitely not suitable for shorter necks.

This neckline has a definite swing to one side. It has to be cut very carefully if you want to create a tailored line that leaves the hair soft and natural with no harsh finishing lines. Razoring could be used to reduce bulk here. Never cut against the dominant swing but allow the natural swing to control the cutting.

This duck-tail growth is controlled by a swing into the centre nape from either side. The razor is the ideal tool for controlling the density in the middle. This style enables the hair to swing in easily from each side.

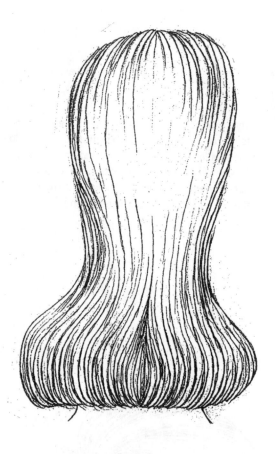

This square shape adds width to the back of the head and can be used to disguise and flatter a long, thin neck. It is also a good shape for anyone who is exceptionally tall.

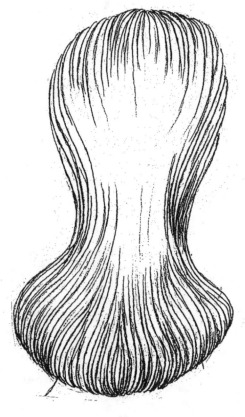

Another version of the longer look, ideal for taller people, has the hair at the back neck line rounder in shape and allows for softer movements at the ends. It can also be used to disguise the broad shoulders of more heavily built people.

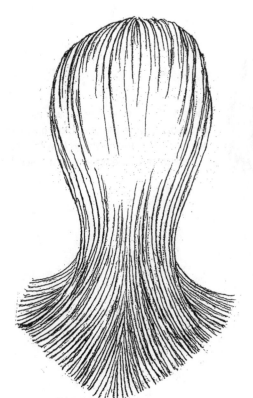

For the taller woman again, with a broader but shorter neck, the oval neck line adds length and narrows the back.

This is a useful variation of the neck line for a person of medium height with a long neck. The triangular V-shape is ideal, adding height to the body as well as the head.

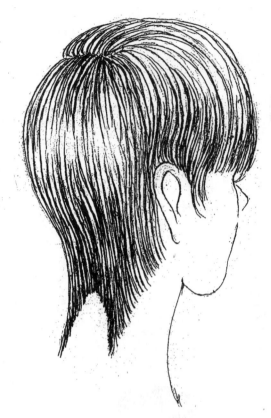

Some hairlines at the nape show a bare area in the centre back, while the sides grow down into low points. This illustration shows how this feature can be made attractive by emphasizing the lack of hair.

This is a good style for a tall person with a long neck. The soft natural drape of hair at the nape can be used to cover any abnormal growth at the roots. Hair that is fine and lank should be left longer and thicker.

 # The basic styles

Applying the basics

The object of this chapter is to show you how to apply the basic rules of cutting and setting to achieve the various shapes and movements that go into the creation of each hair style. A number of classic styles are demonstrated which can be achieved with the use of the basics. Most of them rarely date because they have an uncluttered line which is elegant and lovely to look at. The principle behind these exercises is to make you aware of a cutting plan, while at the same time encouraging you to apply the rules learned. The rules of the road do not change just because you are driving a Rolls Royce instead of a Mini. Similarly, fashions may change, but a good craftsman with a knowledge of the basic skills will know how to adjust to the whims of fashion, now and in the future. Practising, studying and executing lines like these will be an invaluable contribution to your hairdressing experience.

Before you start ...

The fall of hair is controlled principally by the direction in which it grows. If the hair follicles are angled in an awkward direction on the head and nape it causes some distortion at the roots and affects the fall of the hair when dry. Dry hair has a different fall to wet hair. When cutting, make a point of studying the head dry before it is shampooed, especially with longer hair. This will give you a clearer picture of the line and fall of the hair. You may need to leave extra length in some areas where it is needed to compensate for a distortion in the hair growth.

You should also note how much natural elasticity or bend there is in the hair. Most hair has some degree of natural movement like this; rubbing small portions of the damp hair usually gives some indication of any natural curve or bend that will affect the cut and the finished shape. Hair that has too much bend will accentuate any growth distortion at the root and will show up after cutting when it is dry.

The classic turned-under look

The classic turned–under look requires a simple one-length cut with no layering. It is a natural classic cut for most age groups and can be adapted to create many variations. It can be a base for the heavy, fringed bobbed effect, an almost perfect cut for straight and medium fine hair and is also suitable for coarse, heavy-textured hair.

(above and right) The classic turned-under look, also known as the 'page-boy' look.

(left) Another version of the same cut is the heavy-fringed bobbed effect which is also popular. This style can be used to disguise many defects at the hairline and in the nape of the neck. The simple shape can be adapted to provide a number of variations by having different lengths at the back and sides.

The cut

There are three sections of hair to consider; the front, back and sides. In a style like this where the hair length varies it is essential to use a device like the circle method, especially when the face-framing lengths need to be angled precisely.

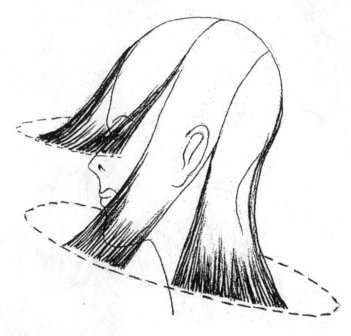

For the front section above the eyes, use the receding points at the temples as a guide. An imaginary circle from the chin sloping downwards to the centre of the nape acts will act as a guideline. The one-two-three sectioning method will enable you to control the bulk of the hair easily during cutting. The accent is on a graceful fall of hair towards the back of the head.

The long hair in the centre has to be cut skilfully to blend with the longer nape hair. All the hair is angled to create a graceful downward shape. Keep the 'circle' in mind, angling it from the chin towards the centre back. Cut a small section in the nape first. Be exact! Use this as the guideline and take successive sections to complete the back. There is no need to take very tiny sections along the back of the head as is sometimes advocated. This is unnecessary and time-wasting unless the hair is abnormally thick. Blend all the lengths into the back using the guideline from the chin. Bevel the points carefully, either holding the hair between the fingers, or using the back of the comb to control the final shaping. The lengths above the eyes and forehead are cut as in the basic procedure, from the two receding points on the temple.

The back

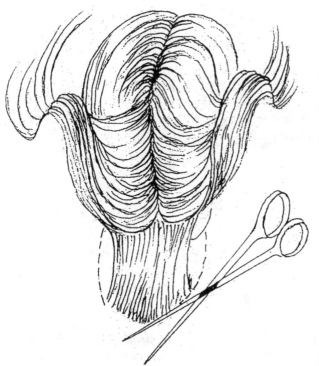

1. Part the hair at the back, down the centre, and separate a small section in the nape to be cut as a guide. Note the direction of the line circling towards the chin, which will be your guideline for successive cutting. The longest hair is in the centre. Be sure the scissors are angled correctly before making any cut.

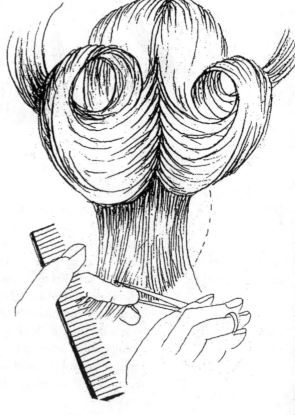

2. The forefinger and middle finger of the left hand control the hair while the cut is made with the right. This will give a neat precise cut at the nape.

3. Once your guideline is cut precisely, take successive sections to complete the cut. When cutting the nape, fingers can be used to control the hair, pressing it into the neck

4. The fingers or the back of the comb can be used to control the hair while cutting the final strands. As this is a one-length cut, it is vital to work with the natural fall of the bulk hair so that it can be cut evenly without excessive pulling at the roots.

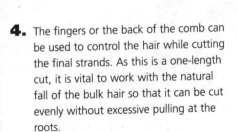

The sides

5. The top lengths are cut last after the side lengths have been blended into the back. The angle of the scissors must be positioned exactly along the guideline of the chin. Finalize the cut by checking and combing the hair into the back lengths to ensure that the sides fall correctly from above the ears.

6. Follow the same procedure on the opposite side of the head, angle the scissors so that they point towards the chin. When cutting the last layer, the hair should be left fractionally longer at the back and sides to help the movement to curve under.

The front

6. Cut a small section taken from the hairline as a guideline for cutting the front section as a fringe which is a popular feature with this style. The remainder can then be trimmed by angling the meshes between the fingers to bevel it into shape.

7. The final bevelling of the ends on the front movement is done to impart a slight layering at the ends of the hair. Notice how the ends are held up at an angle; the more acute the angle, the more layering at the ends. Check and re-check the fringe. Trimming little and often is the best treatment here.

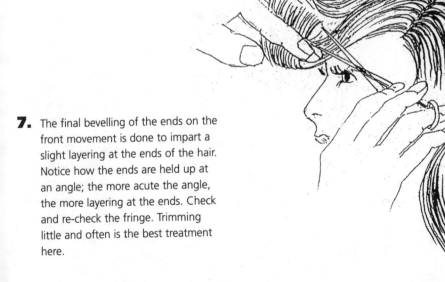

The set

To achieve bounce, bend and body in the hair, roller setting, blow-drying and permanent waving are the usual means of giving movement to the hair. An electric styling iron or heated rollers are sometimes used to give instant bounce to the ends when blow-drying has not created sufficient curve and bend. Just drying and turning under the ends is not enough; the blow-drying operation must control the complete movement of hair, from the roots to the points. The root control required is the same as that for the basic set. The setting pattern shown is used in all variations of this style where the bulk of the hair is turned under. Never stray from this pattern. Each roller is placed with the object of achieving a graceful, curved fall of hair. The final shape is already obvious in the setting – a good example of directional setting.

1. Note the precise positioning of the rollers. Do not be tempted to place any more rollers than shown. The only variation is perhaps on the front of the head where fringe movements may be altered to suit.

2. Never put two rollers where one will do, although you can alter the width of a roller to suit the texture of hair and strength of curve required on the ends. The object of this setting is to achieve a graceful, curved fall of hair. You will never obtain this by cluttering the setting with lots of small rollers.

3. Note how each roller is positioned, just underneath the occipital bone. When the basic brushing movements are carried out the hair will fall naturally into shape without snarling or root partings showing.

Blow-drying

This setting pattern that can be created by blow-drying if necessary. The advantage of this over roller setting is that there are no separations in the hair. This style lends itself to blow-drying principally because it creates a natural free-fall of hair around the bone structure of the head. Follow this standard routine for all heads wanting a page-boy look.

1. (above) You should normally start blow-drying at the back of the head, but sometimes it is a good idea to deal with the fringe while it is still wet; this will enable you to see any slight blemishes in the ends so that they can be bevelled before they are completely dry.

2. (left) The front section in this fringed shape is being stretched over the brush to soften the bend in the ends of the hair. Different brushes create varying degrees of softness or crispness of bend, curl or movement. The choice of brush is up to you; with experience you will be able to select the right brush for the effect you want to create.

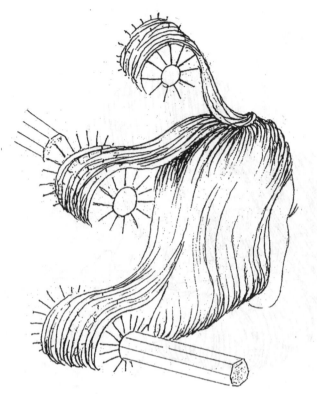

3. Starting at the nape, blow-dry the hair movements. Turn the ends of the hair under while directing the hot air onto the brush. By using hot air and a round brush you can achieve the same effect as a roller would produce. Follow the same order of working as in the cutting procedure.

4. Finalize the side sections and back by wrapping the ends around the brush with the hand. Twist the brush slightly to grip the ends and hold the nozzle of the drier close to the brush. This gives a final crispness and smooth look to the line without any harsh lines and it will enable you to texture the hair with a dressing-out brush (not just any kind of brush!) and achieve that lovely groomed yet natural look.

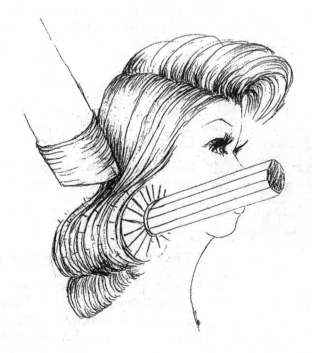

Controlling the ends

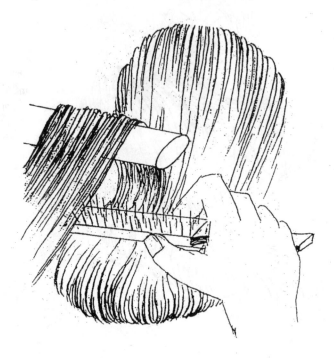

5. When working the brush and blow-dryer together, the barrel of the blow-dryer can be used as shown, to lift the hair to enable the brush to be placed under the movement. With a slight twist of the wrist the brush grips the mesh of hair, the drier is pulled away and the hair is dried. This is repeated until all the movements are dried.

> **Remember**
>
> You are not brushing just to loosen curl, but to produce a movement with shape and line.

Dressing-out

Dressing-out should start with the basic brushing procedure, brushing from side to side thoroughly, relaxing the curve in the ends until the shape falls in naturally.

The layered cut for the frothy look

This style has been chosen because of its classic origin. There is a definite Grecian influence in the overall shape of these seemingly casual yet contrived movements around the head. Many style adaptations come from this line and practising layer cuts such as this will be invaluable.

The frothy look

This lovely frothy look, achieved with a layer cut, is another classic style.

The cut

Length is all–important and you should use the 'circle' guideline for the front, sides and back. The profile below shows the hair slightly shorter at the nape of the neck. The lengths are curved, longer at the front of the head and on the crown, to give a fuller effect in the final brushing. These are subtle touches in a cut that you must teach yourself in order to develop a flair for artistic cutting.

The lengths of the different sections vary as shown here. The hair is shorter at the back and has to be layered into the nape. There is a gradual increase in length towards the front of the head, following the 'circle' guideline.

Having cut the all–round

Remember

The bodying process is not intended to thin the hair or shorten the lengths.

lengths, if the hair density requires it, a slight micro-layering or bodying of the hair should be carried out (see page 54). If executed with great care, bodying will create more body and bounce in the resulting style.

Comb the hair and check and re-check as you direct the hair downward and towards the face, from the pivot-point on the crown to the nape, the top forward to the eyes, and the sides towards the face. Bevel the ends: this must be done thoroughly before the final layering.

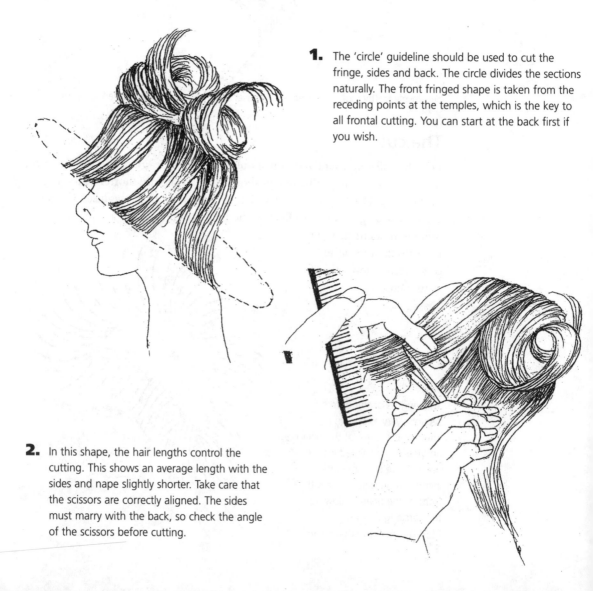

1. The 'circle' guideline should be used to cut the fringe, sides and back. The circle divides the sections naturally. The front fringed shape is taken from the receding points at the temples, which is the key to all frontal cutting. You can start at the back first if you wish.

2. In this shape, the hair lengths control the cutting. This shows an average length with the sides and nape slightly shorter. Take care that the scissors are correctly aligned. The sides must marry with the back, so check the angle of the scissors before cutting.

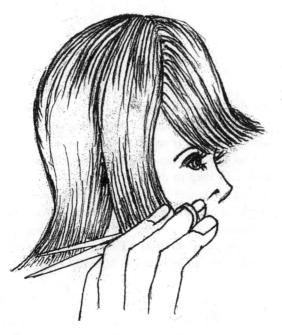

3. This shows the final bevelling cut on the nape hair. The diagram is slightly exaggerated to stress the importance of using the guidelines to blend each section into the next. Comb and re-comb the hair, allowing the fall of the hair to indicate where the final snip at the ends is needed. Any bodying or micro-layering should be done at this stage, if required, without losing any length.

Layering

The hair should now be brushed back away from the face. Follow the layering procedure shown in the diagrams below. Notice that the lengths are somewhat longer in the front and top of the head to give a fuller and bouncier look.

4. Comb all the hair back from the forehead to carry out the layering technique. As in the basic cut, take a line from the centre forehead and cut in the direction shown.

Remember

Scissors should be parallel to the line from the centre forehead to the crown, never across the head.

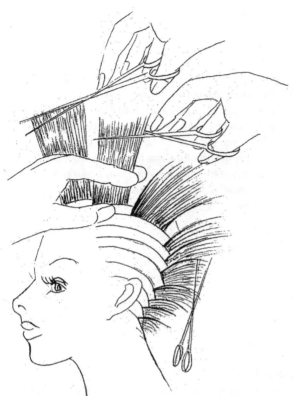

Part the various sections meticulously as you gradually layer the lengths throughout the head. Work from the ear round to the back of the head, first on one side, then the other. Don't be haphazard; keep to the cutting routine. Remember where there are to be different lengths of hair and, visualize the finished result in your mind while cutting – this is how flair develops. Think the shape! Think the length! Think of the angle! Cutting flair will come!

5. (top) Follow the sectioning routine keeping the partings parallel to the imaginary centre line from the nose to the pivot point on the crown and into the centre nape. Never cut across the head! Visualize the various lengths and remind yourself of the angle to cut by repeating to yourself 'Lift the hair and cut at 100 degrees - or 40 degrees, depending on the head.

6. (right) This illustrates the angles of the various lengths at the back of the head. Section the hair neatly and precisely as you gradually layer the lengths. When you reach the sides, angle from the ear to the centre nape and vice versa on the other side of the head. Keep to the cutting shape and obey the rules.

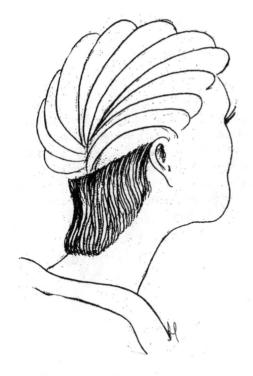

7. This shows the cutting angles at the back of the head and the direction of the cut, not the shortness. The hair at the nape is approximately 5 cms, while the remainder is longer and cut in varying lengths towards the front of the head, to give a bouncy fullness to this pretty, feminine style.

The set

This style normally requires setting to acquire the movement and volume necessary for the final presentation, but on certain heads where the hair has a natural bend, the hair can be left to dry naturally. A combination of perfectly positioned rollers of varying widths, and, if necessary, a few well executed pin-curls can give this layer cut a beautiful freedom of line that will be pleasure to brush when you come to dressing-out. Brush the hair in the usual way, making certain the roots blend well into the movements. Using a fluffing action with the brush, allow the movements to settle freely, especially on the front of the head where the curls should float casually into place. The characteristics of this casual and tousled look can be adapted to many different moods of fashion. Longer hair cut in the same way can be turned into some exciting styles.

This setting shows how a combination of well-positioned rollers of varying widths, perfectly placed, with a few pin-curls at each side can give this layer cut a lovely natural look and a freedom of line which is a pleasure to brush.

Dressing-out

Brush the hair in the usual way, blending the root hair thoroughly into free-flowing movements, without making any final positioning with the brush. This design needs finishing with a delicate fluffing action with the brush to give the springy fullness of the shape at the top and front of the head. Allow the hair to settle naturally and float loosely into place.

The layered cut with a longer look

The basic characteristics of this casual look may be adapted to a variety of styles. Hair a little longer but cut using the same plan, can lead to exciting variations such as this. The sides and back hair are short, but the nape lengths are left longer and blow-dried. Notice the soft wave movements on the sides. Instead of a having a forward movement as in the last dressing, this version is blow-dried back off the face but allowed to bounce softly on to the forehead by means of a little back-brushing at the roots.

The forward look with flick-ups

This style cannot be executed with scissors. Only a razor can produce this cut efficiently and artistically as the razor can cut into the growth direction of the root hair much more subtly than scissors. The point of the razor can also sculpt into a movement directly without disturbing it and therefore has more control in eradicating any distortion. Do remember it is a tool to be used with care. Hold the razor firmly in the hand, controlled and directed by the forefinger and thumb (see page 19).

This head-hugging tailored shape illustrates how well a razor cut can produce a neat, controlled shape at the nape of the neck. In some instances a fold-over or a duck's-tail effect may be created, depending on the growth direction of the hair at the nape.

The tailored look with flick-ups

Here is another instance where a lovely tailored nape shows a sculpted style off to perfection. The hair is drawn straight back off the face in a simple, uncluttered line into the nape, concentrating the attention of the shape at the sides. The cut must be perfect!

The cut

To create this head-hugging shape, the razor must cut into the swing of the hair growth with extreme care and control. The point of the razor must sculpt into a movement without disturbing the natural lie. The razor is used with a short flicking action that sculpts rather than cuts. Leave the natural hairline as it is, but should the neckline hair grow awkwardly you must change the line slightly and adjust it by cutting the hair at the neck line straighter and create a neat curved edge with the scissors.

1. Comb all the hair forward from the crown and cut the guidelines for the front and sides before starting at the nape. Pick up small sections of hair, which have been moulded into their growth direction, between forefinger and thumb of the left hand. With the point of the razor, shape the length with a short flicking action that sculpts the hair.

2. Leave the natural hairline untouched as you continue taking sections, progressively working into the direction of the growth, gradually tailoring the shape. As you progress, remove the bulk from the centre nape, slightly shortening the length at the same time and therefore allowing the side lengths to fold over. Work from side to side with finger and thumb controlling the hair meshes to be cut. Use a slicing action with the point of the razor. Sculpt the shape of the centre nape, followed by the side lengths, before continuing upwards.

3. To ensure that the hairline is left natural, as a precaution, take a fine parting on the outside hairline at the nape and bevel the points carefully with scissors, shortening where necessary, to complete the cutting at the nape. Do this on either side of the nape. It will allow the fold-over to mould into shape easily.

Squared neck for an irregular hairline

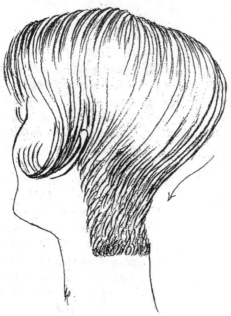

4. Sometimes the growth of the hairline is distorted, by a strong downward pull, for example, in which case the cut must be adapted to follow that distortion. Cut in a downward direction as shown, leaving an attractive fullness which helps to cover up any distortion of root hairs. Cut the ends into a neat edging to suit the neck line and the style.

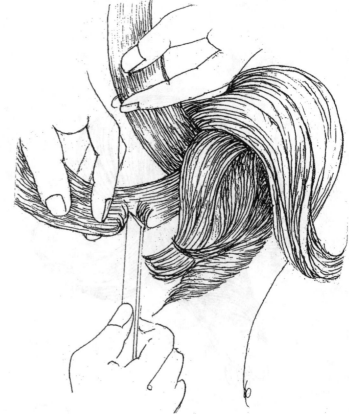

5. As you progress upwards, the hair in the centre nape should be slightly shortened, allowing the fold over, or duck tail, to form. Let the area underneath the occipital bone dictate the shape. Using the slicing action with the razor to reduce the lengths at the back, the front and sides. The next stage is bevelling the ends with the scissors.

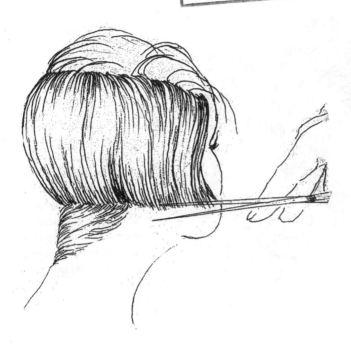

6. Next, comb the hair towards the back and the sides. Comb and re-comb and, following the line of the imaginary circle, bevel the ends of the back and side movements. Check and re-comb the lengths repeatedly during this procedure. This is the only way in which you will get maximum control during the bevelling of the edges.

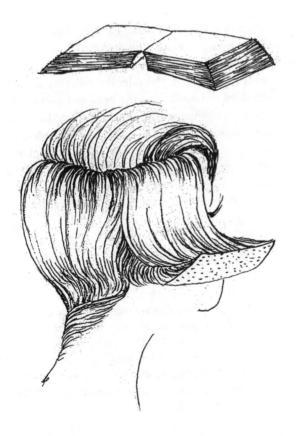

7. Finalize the cut by bevelling a slight layer into the front and sides. The sketch shown has been exaggerated to show what happens when you cut the hair ends at an angle away from the head, either upwards or downwards.at the ends. It is similar to the way the pages spread out when you open a book. The more the sections are lifted away from the head as you cut, the more pronounced the layering will be, resulting in a softer, curlier look.

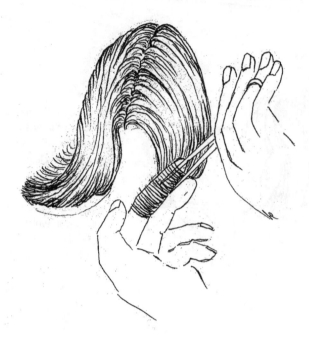

8. It is difficult to define exactly at what angle the hair should be held away from the head as this will vary according to the skill of the cutter, the thickness of the hair, the texture and the shape of the head. The more it is lifted away from the head the softer and curlier will be the final look.

The set

When setting, take care when placing rollers at the back just behind the crown. These are directed downwards to give a lift at the roots. The emphasis is on the front of the head, immediately above the eyes, where the rollers are turned upwards. At the sides the rollering is carefully moulded outwards from the head and into the two curved movements with the ends clipped securely into the stems. This is an example of the controlled moulding of wet hair without disturbing the roots. Although this line can be blow-dried, the setting with rollers creates a better shape because of the need to sculpt the wet hair from the roots which blow-drying does not do.

1. Medium-large rollers are used in this shape, and the sides have two outwards-and-upwards pin-curls. Carefully control the hair at the roots before placing the rollers. For the pin-curls, mould the side movements and turn the ends outwards from the head, then into the curved movement, and clip securely. Scroll the root hair at the nape very carefully.

2. Repeat the procedure on the other side of the head. The rollers are used not to achieve a curl but movement, and subtle lift at the root, on the crown and the back for the final brushing. Again, the scrolling of the hair while wet gives a subtle shape.

Dressing-out

Brush the hair backwards with both comb and brush in the basic procedure. Thoroughly blend the root hair well from side to side, before floating the hair forward into the final shape. Fluff the front with the brush and let it settle naturally. Let the point of the comb deal with any runaway tendrils of hair.

1. Brush the hair backwards to blend the movements thoroughly and efficiently so that the hair will fall into place naturally.

2. If the brushing is executed well you will find
that, as the hair is floated towards the front of
the head with the brush, the shape will settle
naturally in soft, fluffy movements. Let the
brush dictate the action now, with a continual
lifting and floating of the ends. If depth is
wanted, use a slight binding stroke with the
brush.

3. Use the comb to control any tiny, loose whips
of hair and runaway tendrils. Excess pressure
should never be used. Let the point of the
comb, held as shown, direct the wayward
ends into the main shape without flattening
the line and general flow of hair.

twelve

Geometric cutting

The basic techniques, particularly the 'circle' method, provide a sound method of working that will enable you to develop a feeling for cutting and flair in adapting styles to suit the various fashion trends that tend to suddenly appear on the hairdressing scene. The 'circle' method is particularly well suited to geometric cutting for 'straight' styles. The main feature of the geometric look is a natural fall of hair around the head that is precisely cut and not straight, as you might think, but curved! It is a simple one-length cut with no layering or graduation, though lengths may vary and designs differ.

Curve in a head of hair is natural! The illustrations show how the 'circle' lends itself so naturally and easily to the geometric look even though this is usually associated with straightness, solidity and square or triangular cutting. The circle may vary its direction and shape, depending on the natural wave; it can be up at the back, or down. The hair can be cut in varying lengths to create a fringe. Longer hair can be given a solid, sculptured look by having the bulk of the hair draped at the side of the head, contrasting with a short nape. This cut is controlled mainly by the fall of the hair, and achieved by studying the growth direction and the way the head is held, together with angling the scissors correctly. To achieve a soft, natural look in geometric cutting, visualize a landscape stretching into the distance in generous curves and soft shapes, or a blade of grass bending gently in the breeze: compare these images with the way hair falls around the skull in soft shapes before dropping into a natural fall.

The geometric cut

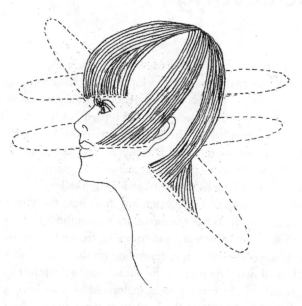

When adapting the basic cut to the geometric look imagine the 'circle' changing direction to act as a guide for the various lengths around the head.

The eventual aim is a natural fall of hair around the head.

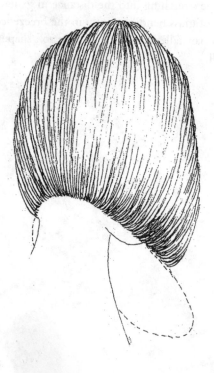

1. The mass of hair at the front of the head contrasts with the short, neatly groomed nape hair but the cut is still guided by the 'circle' method.

Pivot point

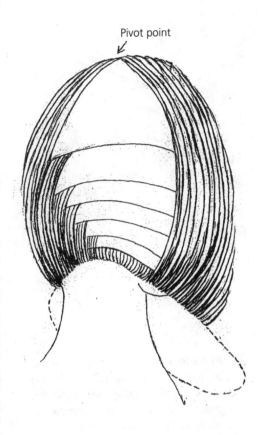

2. The simple pattern of the cut evolves from a series of
partings, starting at the nape and continuing upwards.
The sections can be made larger after the first sections
at the nape have been cut. Care must be taken to find
the growth direction and the natural fall from the
pivot-point on the crown.

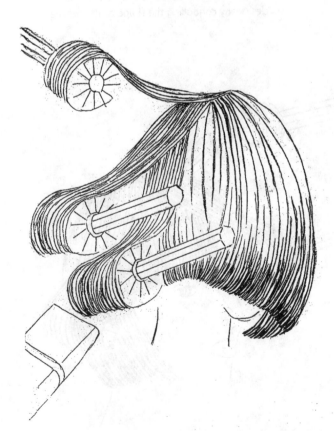

3. This style needs extra care when blow-drying.
Starting at the nape, take sections and work
upwards making certain the root hair is dried
into a good shape. Remember the result is
exactly the same as in setting, even though the
blow-dryer is being used. Don't just think
about the points only: round the movement
from root to point.

The fringed look

1. This heavily fringed look is guided by two imaginary circles clearly controlling the shape of the outline.

2. As the focal point of this style is centred on the forehead it is better to start with the fringe, carefully cutting a few guidelines, then cutting the bulk, sectioning the hair neatly as shown: be very precise.

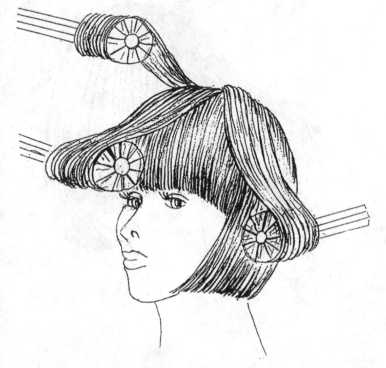

3. This cut must be blow-dried and very carefully moulded into a curved shape. To achieve this simple, beautifully curved, line the brush should be carefully manipulated during the drying so that the resulting groomed style gives the appearance of casual naturalness.

The V-shaped neck line

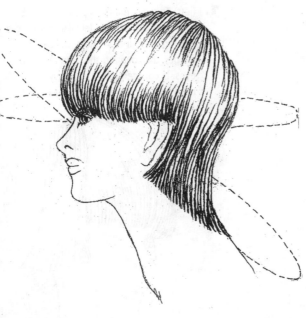

1. (left) This is a variation on the previous shape showing a dramatic deep fringe and a triangular V-shaped neckline, both guided by a circle. The emphasis is on the fringe which is extended beyond the forehead to just behind the ear.

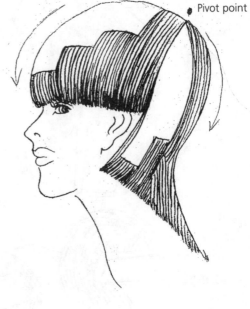

Pivot point

2. (right) The cut can be started either at the nape or at the front of the head. The style is divided into two parts, the front hair and the back hair, separated by a parting from the pivot-point, or crown, to just behind each ear. When finalising the cut, make sure the hair is well moulded from the crown downwards.

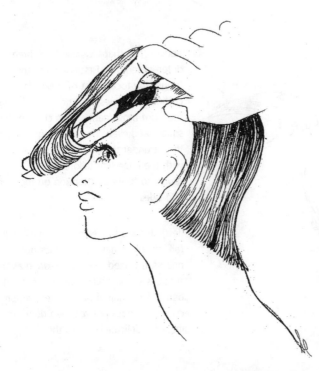

3. (left) For this style the hair is left long and heavy on the top and front of the head to obtain a solid look. Sometimes blow-drying does not give enough bounce, but instant bend can be given using heated irons or a hot brush on the ends.

Short and sweet

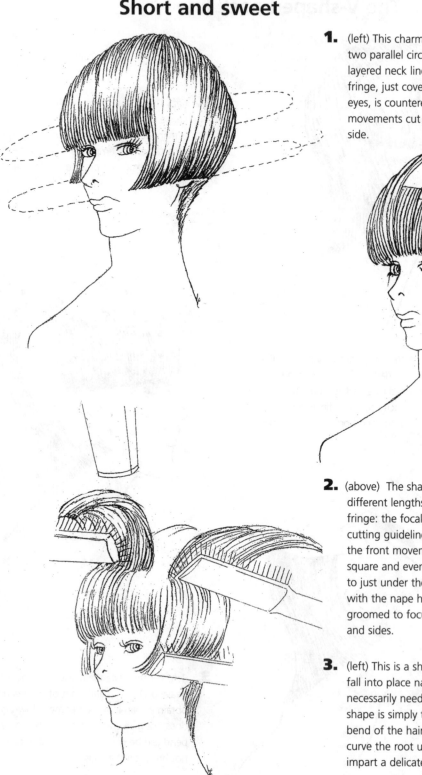

1. (left) This charming shape is guided by two parallel circle guidelines balancing a layered neck line. A short, delicate fringe, just covering the area above the eyes, is countered by the heavy movements cut very square at each side.

2. (above) The shape is based on three different lengths. First complete the fringe: the focal point of this style, cutting guidelines and then completing the front movement. Then cut the sides square and even. The back is graduated to just under the occipital bone area with the nape hair tailored and groomed to focus attention on the front and sides.

3. (left) This is a shape that, cut well, will fall into place naturally. It does not necessarily need to be blow-dried as the shape is simply taken from the natural bend of the hair. If blow- dried, simply curve the root upwards then down to impart a delicate bend to the hair.

A face-framing style

1. (left) This unusual face-framing style again demonstrates the use of the natural 'circle' guideline. The hair from just underneath the ears and at chin level is angled away sharply towards the back into a triangular turned-under effect. Comb and mould the hair correctly before making any cutting strokes. Be sure to mould the hair from the pivot-point on the crown. The bulk will then fall naturally around the head.

2. (top right) Cutting a simple guideline around this hairline can be quite tricky. Let the natural fall around the frontal and temporal bones guide you before cutting. You must get the correct fall around the curve.

3. (below) At the back, find the angle first before cutting the natural line falling from the occipital bone. Be certain the hair hangs naturally and does not drag the root while cutting.

4. (below) Because of length and weight of hair in this style, some textures of hair may resist becoming curved when being blow-dried, but heated irons or a hot brush should be sufficient to give some bounce and curve to the ends.

The rounded geometric look

1. (top left) This is a dramatic, rounded, geometric look, reminiscent of the Cromwellian era when hair was quite severely cut like this. It is also an excellent shape for disguising faults round the hairline on the forehead. The round, downward shape is particularly suitable for faces with the long oval and the long square look.

2. (top right) The cutting plan is quite simple but there is no room for error. No layering is necessary, but the nape hair is tailored to the head by a graduation, using the scissors-over-comb technique (see page 24). The nape should be cut first, then, after cutting a guideline round the perimeter of the rounded shape, cut the remainder of the lengths to that line exactly. Check the cut continuously.

3. (left) To control the ends effectively, use a round brush to lift the roots and dry, turning the points under. Ideally, the rounded shape should be finished off with the hot brush to accentuate the roundness at the ends.

thirteen Long hair

The main problem when first handling long hair is coping with its bulk. At the back of the head this problem can be overcome by dividing the hair into sections and putting it up into a chignon, pleat or Grecian knot. This is a purely mechanical process, like constructing a sculpture over a base – and the base is the key to the problem. Study the following ways of creating a basic structure with long hair and you will be able to adapt it to suit many styles with different lengths.

A simple pleat or fold-over will control and conceal the bulk of hair at the back of the head. The pleat has appeared again and again in hairstyling over the years. It can be executed anywhere on a head.

The chignon, or gathering of hair at the nape is also a classic shape. If you study art or history you will often see the chignon depicted in one form or another, sometimes contained in a net.

Lastly there is also the twist where the mass of hair is controlled and prepared by repeated brushing and twisting of the bulk until the hair is tight to the scalp, where it is secured with pins, with the ends of the hair coiled on top of the head or braided into a loop.

Authors have given us lyrical descriptions of 'wondrously coiled hair' and 'glorious braided strands', while the old masters such as Botticelli, Watteau, Titian, Raphael, etc. painted beautiful hair with recognizable pleats, coils, twists, and chignons.

It is worth taking the time and trouble to learn the routines, permutations and manipulations needed for dealing with long hair as such styles will no doubt always resurface.

The pleat

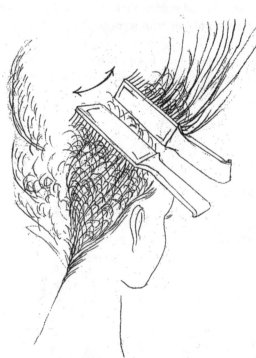

1. (top left) Before dressing the back into a pleat the hair should have some form of bend or movement put in the ends. To start a pleat, part the hair down the centre-back after separating the front section across the top of the head from ear to ear. This front part of the dressing will be completed when the back pleat has been placed and bound in position.

2. (top right) It is important to create a foundation that will control and bind the pleat. To prepare this, first brush the right side away, then take the left section and, with the right hand, fluff up the hair lengths with a brush using a backwards and forwards wrist action. Repeat as necessary along the lengths. This bodied backing will hold the pins and clips that will fix the pleat in place as it is twisted into position.

3. (left) Repeat this for the hair on the right side of the head. This preparation is essential or the pleat will collapse.

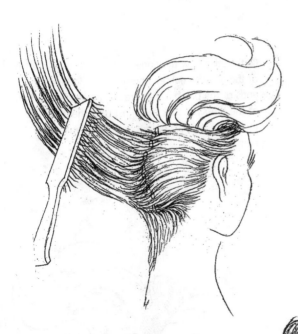

4. (left) Hold all the hair firmly in the left hand and use the brush in the right hand to blend the right section of hair lightly into the rest. You should just stroke the surface hair without destroying the backing. Then give a little backing to the hair just above the ears on each side of the head and blend these into the main shape. The aim now is to lightly smooth and texture the surface hair with the brush. At this point, insert a row of pins to hold the right section and help secure the fold of the pleat.

5. (right) Put in a series of clips as the hair is folded over, turning and tightening it with a twist of the thumb and forefinger. Each clip should be put in neatly and invisibly to secure the fold against the head. The twisting and tightening action will produce a flat, controlled shape from the nape to the crown.

6. (left) At the top of the movement, just on the crown where the bulk of the pleat is to be held, an extra forceful twist of the forefinger and thumb will tighten the fold a little closer to the head. Secure it with a clip. Place one or two strong pins at this point, while the left hand is still holding the pleat in position. You must now make certain that the bulk of the movement is securely pinned to the binding at the roots.

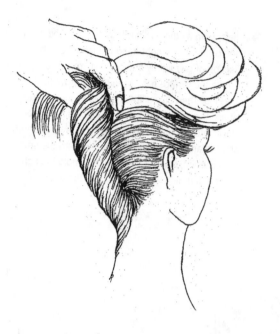

7. (left) Notice how the finger and thumb twist the fold of the pleat to tighten and secure it. To hide the ends of the pleat, if they are not being used as part of the dressing, tuck them just underneath or inside the top of the fold before finally tightening and pinning it.

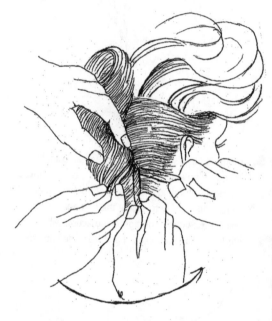

8. (above) To tighten and secure the pleat further, place a series of fine pins up the length of the fold. Hold the pin in the right hand, between your thumb and forefinger, pointing the pin towards the right ear. As you slide the pin into the edge of the pleat, twist the pin over so that it points towards the left ear creating a pull which will give firm control of the hair.

9. (left) Smooth the movement at the back with the brush to subdue any unruly ends. Then dress the top hair at the front. For this style the hair is lightly back-brushed to give the front a softly fringed, frothy shape to contrast prettily with the sleek, groomed look at the back.

The chignon

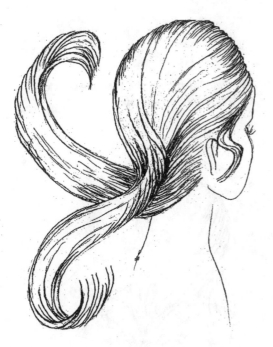

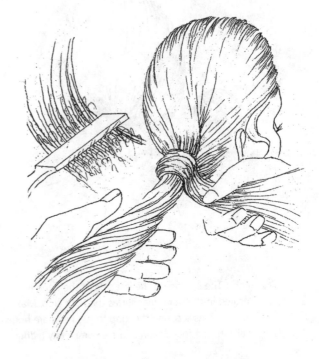

1. (top left) You can create a pretty chignon style in longer hair that is not too strong or forceful, is of medium texture and is resilient. Brush and smooth the general bulk before dividing it into two separate sections. Slip a light elastic band over each section to facilitate easy handling. Cross the sections over – right underneath the left – and secure the knot with one or two strong clips in the nape. Leave a small mesh of hair just in front of each ear to be dressed last, either as a separate drape or to disguise any drag as the main shape is being done.

2. (top right) Both sections of hair should fluffed up using a few binding strokes with the brush. This technique is much kinder to hair than back-combing as it does not knot hair into the roots. Instead, it creates a feathery network that binds the hair in each section together so that they can be manipulated into shape.

3. (left) Once the two sections have some binding the hair can be looped and the curve held against the nape, secured by a clip fixed across the loop (see picture inset).

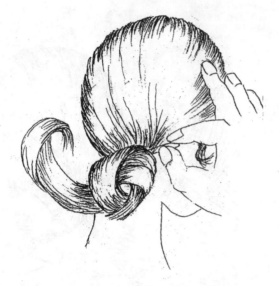

4. (left) Insert more pins to secure each loop thoroughly to the nape.

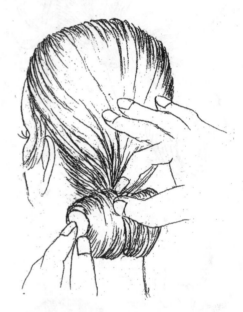

5. (right) The section on the left side of the nape is secured in the same manner as the right side. Make sure the pins securing the loop to the head are hooked well into the foundation and are completely hidden.

6. Before continuing further, neaten up the coils. The side sections can now be fixed into the main shape. Check the overall shape before completing the dressing.

7. (left) Conceal the ends by pinning them into the loop itself. This is open to many variations depending upon the thickness and length of the hair. They are usually be done by pinning the points securely into the nape. Tidy up any stray hairs.

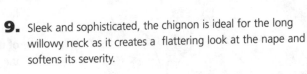

8. (above) To balance the chignon, secure the two loops together in the centre. This is done by using pins in the same manner as was used to tighten the fold-over in the pleat.

9. Sleek and sophisticated, the chignon is ideal for the long willowy neck as it creates a flattering look at the nape and softens its severity.

The twist

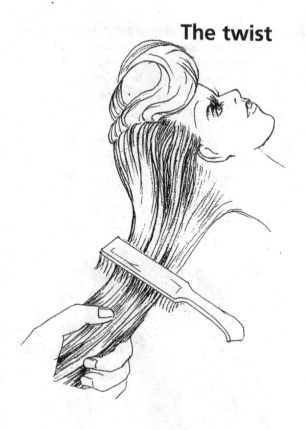

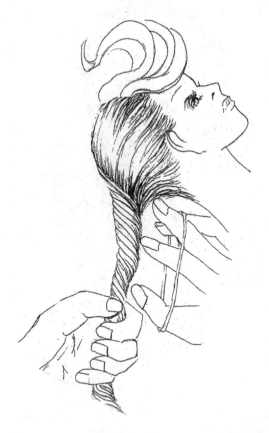

1. (top left) One of the most romantic and simple styles for long hair is this variation of the 'twist' or 'Granny's Knot'. It is particularly suitable for a good hairline at the back of the neck. The hair should be of medium texture. You will find that thick-textured hair has a will of its own, so is not suited to this treatment.

Part the hair across the front of the head just in front of the ears. Take the bulk of the remaining hair and brush, smoothing the surface hairs well, at the same time directing the brushing upwards from the nape to the crown.

2. (top right) A slight binding in the centre of the twist could be used to stiffen the main mass of hair. Any substance such as lacquer or gel could be used for additional support. Continually twist the hair until it is tight against the head, then pull it through a strong elastic band, without releasing the twist.

3. (left) Apply some lacquer or gel along the length to hold and thicken the texture of the movement. As you tighten the twist, secure the ends to the back of the head with self- binding tape which will keep the shape secure.

4. (top left) The front can now be dressed by lightly back-binding the fringe to create a lovely deep, curved shape over the forehead. Blend the remainder of the side hair into the main shape. A small ornamental flower can be arranged to cover any blemish or tape used to secure the loop to the head.

5. (top right) In this variation the fringe has been developed into a curled and waved movement, delicately contrasting with the groomed back. The flower and ribbon arrangement placed around the elastic not only disguises it but helps secure the ends.

6. (left) The twist is extremely versatile. This elegant and sophisticated hairstyle is easily adapted from the previous look by simply taking away the fringe and sweeping the hair into the back shape, leaving the front of the head smooth and uncluttered.

The knot

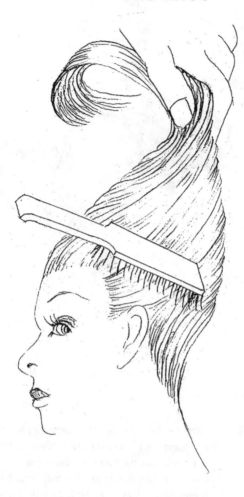

1. Another variation of the twist is the knot. This simple yet elegant shape is most suitable for younger people with a head of hair that lends itself to this kind of manipulation.

Hold all the hair firmly in the left hand and, in an upward direction, brush the hair thoroughly through to the points. Obtain good control of the surface hair by smoothing it with the brush before embarking on the next procedure.

2. When you are satisfied that you have a controlled textured surface, twist the hair continuously until the entire movement is tightly bound by the twist

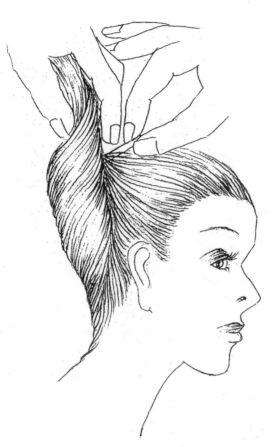

3. Hold the shape very taut at this stage, using you fingers and thumb. This is the point of balance, where two or three substantial pins will hold the mass of hair very firmly. Use the same technique for inserting the pins as in the pleat.

4. Twist the free ends into a knot, tuck the ends underneath, and secure the knot to the base with a series of fine hairpins around the bottom. This should be sufficient to give further security, enabling the client to wear the style confidently, knowing that it will not topple.

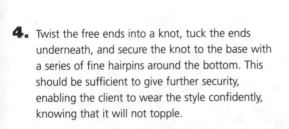

 The style gallery

Linking the basic techniques

All the basic techniques of styling have now been covered: the method of working, basic cuts, setting and dressing-out.

Nature provides natural guidelines to use when creating beautiful styles with precise cuts: the receding points at the temple that define the 'circle' on the head; the hairline to guide a cut; the occipital bone at the back to control a shape or line. The key area lies between the eyes, bordered by the two receding points on either side of the head. This is where a hairstyle starts. This is where we think: does the hair go back, should it have a parting, a side parting, or a forward fringe. From then on it is simply a matter of keeping to a routine and maintaining a planned, well-disciplined way of working.

To re-cap, the very first rule of the 'basics' to remember is the divisions of the head, starting from the receding points on the forehead. These provide the circle plan for setting and cutting. This can be adapted, in geometric cutting, for example, where the circle method is used to blend in the severe fringe movements with the overall shape.

The following illustrations show how easily and naturally the basics can be linked to produce differing styles. Simple classical shapes have been used with soft flattering lines from which can spring many more complicated styles including those used in presentation hairdressing for shows.

The classic one-length style

1. (left) The outstanding feature of this lovely one-length style is the flicked-up ends of the hair which frames the face with the soft, natural drape of hair around the temples.

2. (above) The cutting for this one-length style must start at the back of the head. As always, have the circle and the eventual shape in mind. The line is simple, but it needs skilful and careful cutting. Take a section in the nape and cut a neat line of hair right around the nape.

3. (right) The most important thing at this stage is to achieve a precise finish on the ends. This will create a perfect drop on the outer perimeter of the cut. Hold the strip of hair quite firmly, but do not stretch or pull the mesh of hair. Take care when blending the sides with the nape hair already cut. Always keep your guideline in mind and remember to angle your scissors correctly.

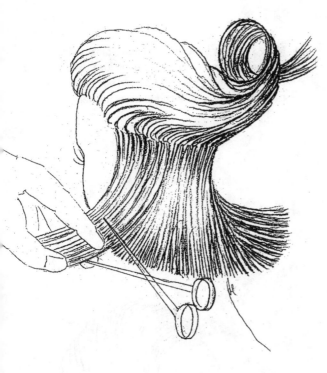

4. (left) Mould the hair while cutting the round of hair at the nape. Comb and re-comb to be certain that these first lengths are evenly cut. Ensure the hair-fall is natural and that there are no distorted twists in the meshes as this will reflect in the final result.

5. (right) Now start blending the remainder of the hair into the nape hair. As each section is taken, comb the hair several times to prepare it for cutting. It is not necessary to measure each mesh of hair, provided it is not too bulky and can be cut precisely.

6. (left) You must patiently follow the basic cutting procedure, as it is in these bold simple cuts that errors show. Taking successive meshes from the top of the head, take care that each mesh is combed and placed correctly, following the natural fall into the nape before cutting. The accent is now on neatness and accuracy as each section is cut.

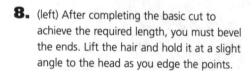

7. Make sure that there are no unruly points suddenly appearing as you comb. It is a good idea to re-check by carefully combing the bulk hair and edging the ends carefully before proceeding to bevel the hair.

8. (left) After completing the basic cut to achieve the required length, you must bevel the ends. Lift the hair and hold it at a slight angle to the head as you edge the points.

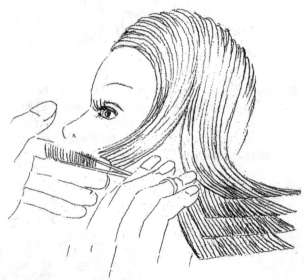

9. This shows another view of the correct cutting angle for bevelling this cut, which is approximately 40 degrees. It is difficult to give a precise angle as this could vary from head to head. Texture and thickness can also affect the amount of bevel needed. You will learn to judge the correct angle with experience.

10. (left) This is the setting pattern for this particular shape. Notice the exact placing of rollers on the top to achieve a lift and bounce on each side of the parting.

11. (above) Brush the hair well to eradicate any excess bounce on the ends. Then use the brushing movements to control the curve and distribute the bulk around the head, creating a soft natural shape. Provided the hair has been cut creatively and precisely, the shape will now emerge as brushing brings the style to life.

12. (left) The hair may have sufficient bounce and elasticity to enable it to be blow-dried into the shape. Using the blow-drying brush, mould the hair upwards, turning it as the jet of air is directed on to the mesh of hair. Hold the brush in position for a few seconds to let the hair cool and set.

13. The outwards and upwards movement is obtained by skilled use of the brush. Hold the brush firmly to brush through the bulk as shown, let the brush dig slightly into the roots just under the occipital bone at the back, then pull the brush outwards and upwards (not too quickly) to form the soft flicked-up curve in the ends.

The long, wavy look

1. This flattering, long cut creates a very feminine look. It has to be skilfully cut if the varying lengths of hair with some natural bend are to allow the movements to fall into place easily. Hair weight can dominate the natural movement, especially on heads that are thick and heavy. You must also keep a lookout for distortions and dominant twists at the hairline.

2. (left) The circle, radiating from the receding points on both sides of the temples, dictates the top. The diagram illustrates the remainder of the head, the prepared plan of the guidelines and the cut of the outline shape. A ring of hair of various lengths around the face is the objective.

3. (above) This shows an outline of the layering procedure and an approximation of hair lengths over the top of the head. The partings run parallel to an imaginary line from the pivot-point on the crown to the centre forehead. The back of the head shows the plan of the partings from the crown to the nape for layering the longer lengths.

4. (left) Having separated the top hair, start cutting at the front. Hold the hair firmly; do not pull. Cut a few hairs as a guideline to cut the front sections. Study the growth direction and if there are any distortions in the natural fall, allow for this during cutting.

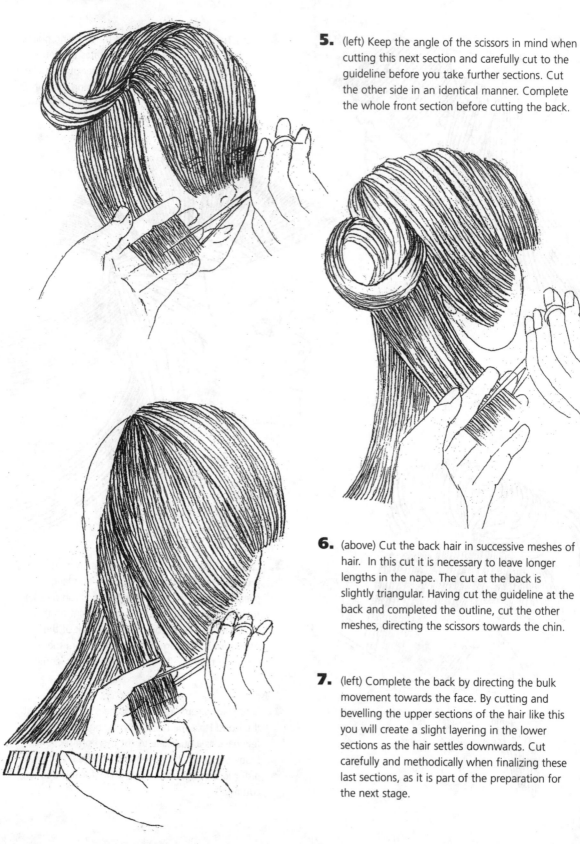

5. (left) Keep the angle of the scissors in mind when cutting this next section and carefully cut to the guideline before you take further sections. Cut the other side in an identical manner. Complete the whole front section before cutting the back.

6. (above) Cut the back hair in successive meshes of hair. In this cut it is necessary to leave longer lengths in the nape. The cut at the back is slightly triangular. Having cut the guideline at the back and completed the outline, cut the other meshes, directing the scissors towards the chin.

7. (left) Complete the back by directing the bulk movement towards the face. By cutting and bevelling the upper sections of the hair like this you will create a slight layering in the lower sections as the hair settles downwards. Cut carefully and methodically when finalizing these last sections, as it is part of the preparation for the next stage.

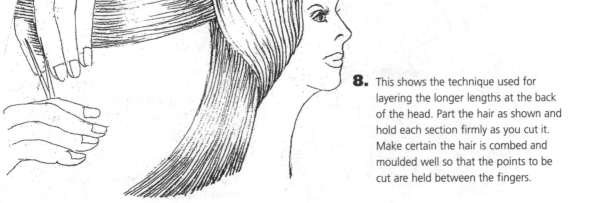

8. This shows the technique used for layering the longer lengths at the back of the head. Part the hair as shown and hold each section firmly as you cut it. Make certain the hair is combed and moulded well so that the points to be cut are held between the fingers.

9. This is the cutting and layering plan at the back of the head. Note the direction and partings of the cut on the lower lengths and the sides of the head.

10. For the final cutting on the top of the head a basic layering routine is used. Part the sections parallel to the line on top of the head. The scissors, too, should always be parallel to this guideline, never across the head.

11. This kind of styling is deceptively casual, the secret lying in the setting of the hair as shown here, with every curve and movement planned before placing. The sizes of the rollers can be varied and the placings adjusted to suit a particular head of hair. Should you wish the result to be very soft, use larger rollers; if a curlier, bouncy look is required, use smaller ones.

12. The principal function of the brush is to reduce tension in the curl and movement. Each brush stroke must begin at the front and finish at the nape or the side of the nape. When the brushing has been rigorous enough throughout the mass of hair and it looks textured and blends easily with no snarl, then the hair is ready to be finalized and presented.

13. The blending and brushing at the nape should be from one side to the other. This will reduce curl tension and blend the separate sections of the setting together to give soft, pliable movements which form the basis of this pretty and feminine look.

14. A casual-looking hairstyle and shape is very deceptive. To achieve this, a knowledge of controlled dressing-out is needed using a wrist action to produce fluffing or back-binding which bonds the hair movements together.

A head-hugging, tousled look

1. (left) This short style has a beautiful line where the bulk hair, swept into the nape, has been cut and sculpted with scissors and razor to create a head-hugging shape, acting as a perfect foil for the casual, tousled look at the front of the head.

2. (bottom left) As the hair is cut shorter on top, it should be well lifted and blow-dried from the root upwards, as shown here. Take short meshes at a time and turn the ends well with a round brush to give maximum bounce.

3. (bottom right) Should a little more 'bite' be needed in the curl, here is a simple but very effective setting plan. Well brushed and controlled it will give the same soft, natural result.

4. Alternatively, heated irons can be used to give instant curl at the dressing-out stage, producing more crispness at the ends.

The straight, forward look

Here is another version of the same look. In this instance the hair has a strong pull towards the forehead and, as the roots have a definite bend, the hair has to be blow-dried and moulded with the fingers.

The asymmetric look

1. (left) This neat, simple shape has an asymmetrical line with a parting. It lends itself particularly well to a head where the hairline has a dominant swing to one side or the other. Quite a complex technical cutting procedure is needed to execute this kind of style.

2. (above) Here is a plan of the cut for you to keep in mind as you cut. The nape hair must be sculpted first with the razor and, when necessary, the bulk hair at the sides and underneath the crown should be roughly shaped and shortened. To complete this bold, asymmetric shape, the back and sides must be finished using the scissors-over-comb cutting technique (see page 24).

3. (left) Here are the three basic working areas: top, sides and nape. The circle guides the movement on the top of the head; the side view shows the layering pattern to be followed in the cut; and the section in the nape is moulded and cut with the razor.

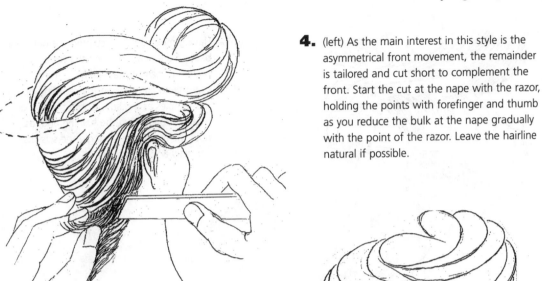

4. (left) As the main interest in this style is the asymmetrical front movement, the remainder is tailored and cut short to complement the front. Start the cut at the nape with the razor, holding the points with forefinger and thumb as you reduce the bulk at the nape gradually with the point of the razor. Leave the hairline natural if possible.

5. (right) Work with gentle stabbing strokes, never forcing the razor, but guiding it. Comb the remainder of the nape hair into the centre. Let the razor sculpt the movement, the fingers controlling the ends as the razor cuts. Softly stroke with the razor rather than using force. It is the density of hair in the centre that needs to be controlled most, to achieve the neat, sculpted look at the nape.

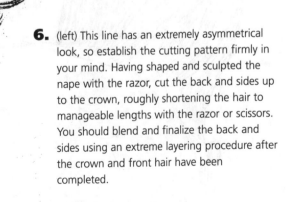

6. (left) This line has an extremely asymmetrical look, so establish the cutting pattern firmly in your mind. Having shaped and sculpted the nape with the razor, cut the back and sides up to the crown, roughly shortening the hair to manageable lengths with the razor or scissors. You should blend and finalize the back and sides using an extreme layering procedure after the crown and front hair have been completed.

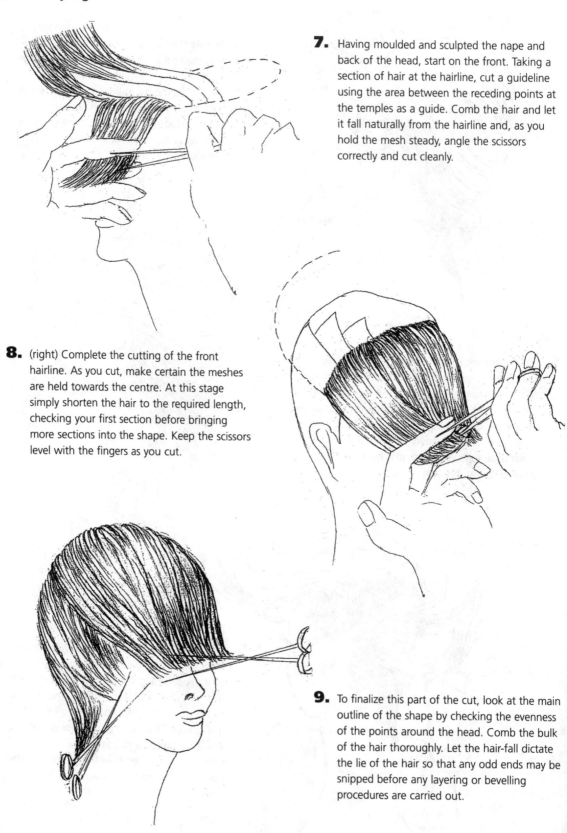

7. Having moulded and sculpted the nape and back of the head, start on the front. Taking a section of hair at the hairline, cut a guideline using the area between the receding points at the temples as a guide. Comb the hair and let it fall naturally from the hairline and, as you hold the mesh steady, angle the scissors correctly and cut cleanly.

8. (right) Complete the cutting of the front hairline. As you cut, make certain the meshes are held towards the centre. At this stage simply shorten the hair to the required length, checking your first section before bringing more sections into the shape. Keep the scissors level with the fingers as you cut.

9. To finalize this part of the cut, look at the main outline of the shape by checking the evenness of the points around the head. Comb the bulk of the hair thoroughly. Let the hair-fall dictate the lie of the hair so that any odd ends may be snipped before any layering or bevelling procedures are carried out.

10. Create a slight layering on the front lengths by lifting the hair up from the head in sections. This layering procedure is not intended to shorten but merely to give a little layering on the ends to create more bounce.

Remember:
Keep the scissors parallel to the line from the nose to the centre point on the crown.

11. For the final bevelling procedure, comb all the front hair down towards the eyes. Comb and re-comb each section before cutting. Be methodical: the bevelling at the ends should not shorten but simply finalize the shape through minimal edging of the points.

12. A little safety procedure to follow to counter loose ends at the hairline is to take a very fine parting all along the hairline at the sides and behind the ears. Comb these towards the face and snip just a slight edging along the points. This will allow the hairline to fit snugly, especially at the nape.

Again, comb a thin mesh of hair from the front hairline and edge the points carefully. This will enable the front edge to be tailored into the shape more easily and control any stray ends.

13. Continue the cut by completing the crown section. Cut the hair in sections, bearing in mind it must blend with the short hair at the nape and sides. Check the angle of the scissors as you layer so that the shorter lengths are directed in towards the nape.

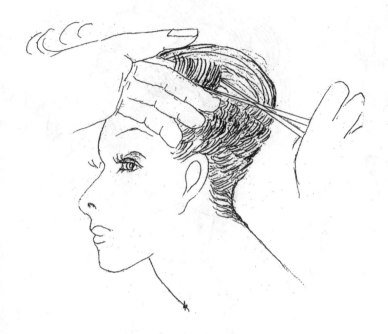

14. Cut the sides by holding the hair between the fingers as shown. This is the most convenient way in which to control the cutting. Keep cutting parallel to the line at the centre of the head from nose to the crown, as you layer the sides of the head.

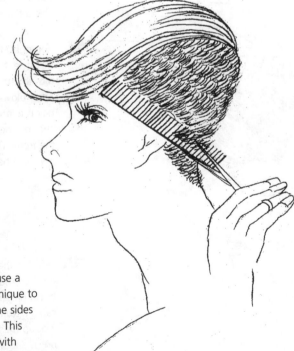

15. It may be necessary to use a scissors-over-comb technique to finalize the cutting of the sides and back (see page 24). This special finish executed with precision will create this bold look.

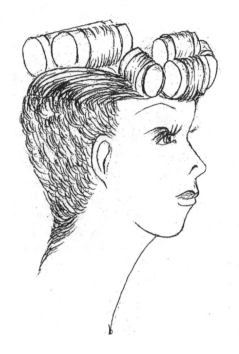

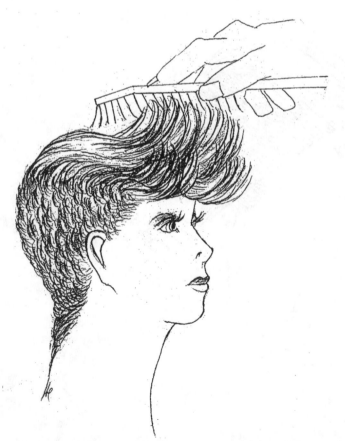

16. (top left) The plan of the setting shows how each roller is placed to achieve a definite shape. The moulding of the sides, back and nape follow the line to give a flattering finish to an excellent cut.

17. (top right) It is quite simple to blow-dry this style if the hair has some natural movement. The method is similar to other blow-drying techniques but, as the hair is a little longer, it is likely that some curl may be necessary to give support to the front. The hot brush or the heated irons can be used to achieve this.

18. (left) For the dressing-out, having brushed the hair thoroughly, let the brush present the final shape; only then can a natural, textured look be created. Pick up the hair movement with the brush and allow the ends to float into the shape easily.

The V-shaped forward look

19. A lovely variation of this cut is to simply carry the cut up the head, leaving the V- shape at the front to create the focal point at the forehead.

The swept-back, long look

1. Designed for long necks and taller women with very long hair, this soft and very feminine look is particularly suited to anyone who wants a definite style rather than a wild, tousled effect. This line is easily managed and, in its many variations, lends itself to permanent waving for those whose hair is resistant to curling when blow-dried.

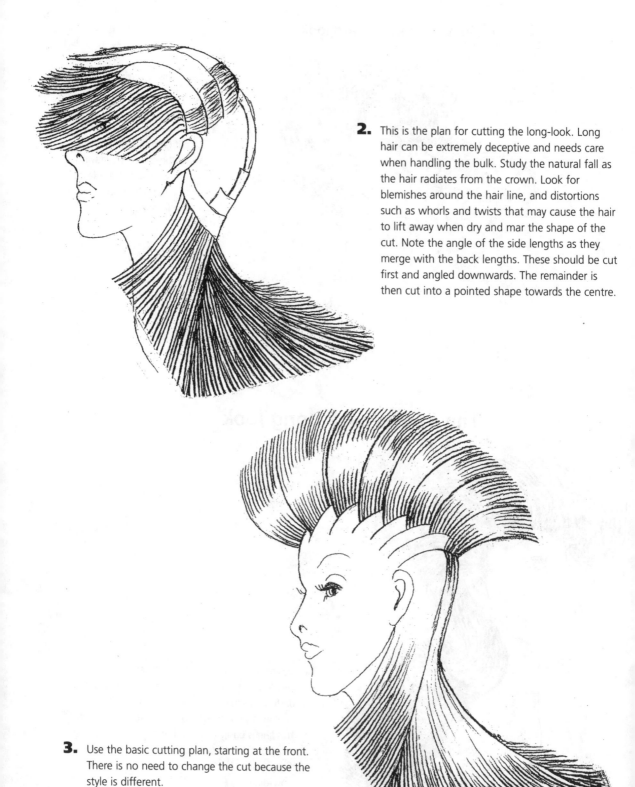

2. This is the plan for cutting the long-look. Long hair can be extremely deceptive and needs care when handling the bulk. Study the natural fall as the hair radiates from the crown. Look for blemishes around the hair line, and distortions such as whorls and twists that may cause the hair to lift away when dry and mar the shape of the cut. Note the angle of the side lengths as they merge with the back lengths. These should be cut first and angled downwards. The remainder is then cut into a pointed shape towards the centre.

3. Use the basic cutting plan, starting at the front. There is no need to change the cut because the style is different.

4. Having cut the front outline, cut the side sections next. Cut in a downwards direction which will give the longer hair lengths its particular shape in the final dressing. The back should then be cut carefully, moulding it into a triangular shape at the centre.

5. Bevel the ends to enable a flicked-back look to be created when blow-drying. Execute this very carefully by lifting the meshes away from the head and bevelling successive meshes at the sides into the centre back.

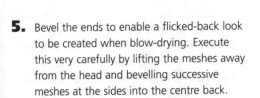

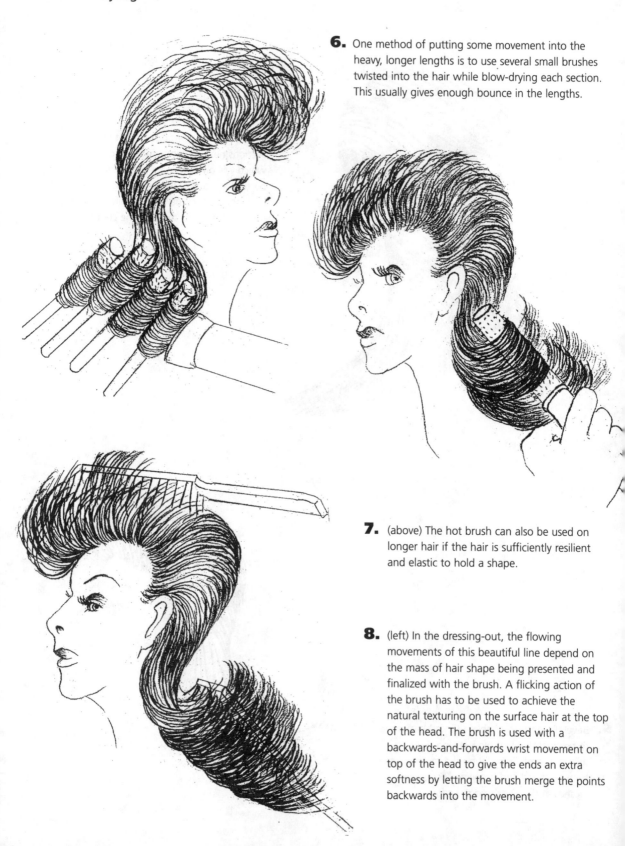

6. One method of putting some movement into the heavy, longer lengths is to use several small brushes twisted into the hair while blow-drying each section. This usually gives enough bounce in the lengths.

7. (above) The hot brush can also be used on longer hair if the hair is sufficiently resilient and elastic to hold a shape.

8. (left) In the dressing-out, the flowing movements of this beautiful line depend on the mass of hair shape being presented and finalized with the brush. A flicking action of the brush has to be used to achieve the natural texturing on the surface hair at the top of the head. The brush is used with a backwards-and-forwards wrist movement on top of the head to give the ends an extra softness by letting the brush merge the points backwards into the movement.

The swept-back look for short hair

1. The same cut as the long-look can be adapted to a much shorter head of hair with a suitable texture and natural bend. The ends at the front and back were layered and bevelled fractionally more than in the longer look to create the two variations shown here.

2. This style can either be blow-dried, or created using this setting plan.

3. Brushed well, the shape is left in the soft, natural movements created by the setting or blow-drying. No back-brushing is necessary.

A face-framing version

4. An alternative style that can be created with the same cut can be blow-waved to create a face-hugging line with the flicked-up ends framing the forehead.

fifteen Abnormalities and treatments

Some abnormalities of the hair

Acne vulgaris This is normally associated with adolescence and is an inflammatory disease of the sebaceous glands in the area of the face, back and chest. In severe cases the skin appears coarse and greasy with some eruptions showing pimples and blackheads where pores are blocked. *Acne papulos*, has blackheads which have developed into reddish pimples. If neglected these may form yellow heads, known as *Acne pustulosa*, which is very infectious and should be treated medically.

Alopecia   A technical name for hair loss or baldness. There are a several varieties:

Alopecia areata is seen as baldness in small circular and oval patches usually at the back of the head. No real reason is apparent, although it has been suggested that an emotional upset can precipitate it. In some instances the patches may be covered with a fine lanugo down with hairs that are thicker at the points surrounding the edges. These 'exclamation hairs', are so called because they look like exclamation marks. The hair usually grows back normally after a time.

These conditions are usually not contagious or infectious, but hairdressers should not attempt to treat any of them: refer the client to the doctor. Even without treatment, in some instances the hair will grow back after about four to six months, but without colour. Nervous diseases and glandular malfunction of the body may be contributing factors.

Alopecia totalis   In some cases the patches become larger and join up forming large areas of baldness. In certain circumstances all the hair from the head and even the eyelashes and eyebrows fall out.

Alopecia universalis   The hair falls out from all over the body.

Diffuse alopecia   Thinning of the hair that sometimes goes unnoticed in the salon, and is often due to a psychological problem. The hair falls out or is shed naturally. This can happen to some women during pregnancy or soon after childbirth, or it can occur as a result of chemotherapy. More often it is caused through illness of a prolonged nature, anaemic conditions, or the damaging effects of drugs. Usually these cases require normal salon services such as shampooing, cutting and styling, as a therapy to bolster the ego, and perhaps to help strengthen weaknesses in the hair growth. Any chemical process should be considered with extreme caution.

Male pattern alopecia refers to the receding pattern of baldness at the temples that happens to men at some time in their life.

Traction alopecia is quite prevalent today but often sufferers, because of vanity and personal pride, refuse to acknowledge it. The symptoms are very visual: there is a sparseness of hair at the root in certain areas of the head. Children often develop this condition, especially teenagers with long hair who have a nervous habit of pulling and twisting the hair which eventually creates a bare patch. This can also occur when single hairs are placed in the mouth and pulled with the teeth. Recovery is usual when the habit is stopped. It can also result from some styling procedures that involve prolonged traction, such as plaiting and braiding routines.

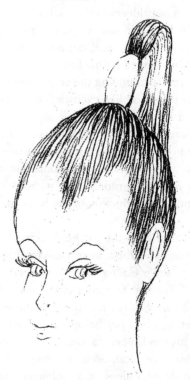

Traction alopecia:

Severe pulling and tight control of the hair at the crown creates a persistent drag at the hair roots around the temples. This will eventually produce the 'M look'.

Canities   The Latin name for greying of the hair. This is a normal process, generally starting at about 30 to 40 years of age, caused by a lack of coloured pigment production. It can occur earlier, making individual hairs white and is a defect rather than a disease.

Cysts When associated with the scalp area or face these are described as sebaceous cysts or wens. They are caused by blockages in the ducts from the sebaceous gland to the follicle. The sebum builds up inside the gland and forms a hard lump in the skin which can grow from the size of a pea to that of a small apple. Although they are not infectious or contagious, surgery is necessary for their removal.

Eczema A redness or inflammation of the skin which can be dry or moist: sometimes seen as swelling, small spots filled with serum, causing a burning sensation with intense irritation. At times areas can be thickened and encrusted and become infected. Certain hairdressing products may cause it to flare up so should not come in contact with sensitive skin.

Fragilitas crinium, or Artefactus The hair shaft is brittle and the ends are usually fractured. The cuticle layer is frayed and often split along the length. The cause is usually harsh chemical treatment, possibly during tinting, bleaching or perming procedures. Treatment is good cutting and conditioning.

Hyperthichosis or Hirsuties Excessive or abnormal growth of hair in areas not usually covered, or even all over the body. The causes can be an abnormal function of the body system which affect hair growth. It can occur in women at some time during their lifetime, due to malfunction of the body system. It is often seen on the upper lips and sides of the face where the lanugo type of hair stiffens and develops into moustache and beard-like forms. Removal requires specialized treatment such as electrolysis.

Molilethrix The hair shaft is alternately swollen and beaded along the length. The cause is an irregular malfunction of the papilla. The beads are known as follicular papules, or pimples. Hair breakage occurs near the scalp.

Pediculosis An infestation of lice (see below).

Pili annulati (ringed hair) A rare form of canities in which the hair shafts shows alternate bands of normally pigmented and lighter hair every millimetre or so.

Pili torti The hair shafts are flattened and twisted so the hair breaks off easily at any point.

Pityriasis Shedding of small scales of skin, basically dead skin cells, referred to as *dandruff* when excessive. Most people have it at some time. It is not contagious or infectious, but if neglected, an unclean scalp can develop *pityriasis steatiodes* (oily dandruff).

Pityriasis steatiodes (oily dandruff) The skin gives off an oily serum which makes the shed scales greasy so that they stick to the skin and hair. If allowed to continue the scalp could be covered with a mass of yellowish brown scales. In this condition the scalp can become infected.

Poliosis Localized whitening of the hair: e.g. a white streak while the rest of the hair remains normal. This can happen in cases of recovery from alopecia areata. The eyebrows and eyelashes can also be affected.

Seborrhoea Caused by an overactive sebaceous gland which produces excessive greasiness of the skin and hair. It is often referred to as seborrhoeic *aleasa* or *scurf* and appears as large greasy skin cells. The condition can be caused by ill health, diet or adolescence, and may be aggravated by bacterial infection. It can be associated with *acne*, causing blackheads. If the hair is just greasy, a simple shampoo treatment can be used, but if any inflammation is seen, the scalp is infected and requires special treatment.

Seborrhoea sicca The common condition of scaliness of the scalp known as dandruff.

Trichorrhexis nodosa Nodes form in the hair shaft due to swelling of the cortex which breaks into threads. The breaks give the appearance of two shaving brushes pressed together.

The important of pH in hair conditioner

The pH of a solution is the degree to which it is acid or alkaline. At pH 7 a solution is neutral. Hair, skin and nails are mildly acidic when they are normally healthy, but if the protective acid mantle is disturbed by a high alkaline solution, some structural damage can occur. Hair is normally exposed to the action of the natural oils and secretions of sebaceous and sweat glands which coat the hair to form this acid 'liquid mantle'. This can also be formed artificially. During the course of some normal hairdressing processes, such as permanent waving, bleaching and tinting, the pH value is slightly above 9 which means that they coat the hair with an alkaline liquid mantle. Traces of these materials can remain both in and on the hair even after shampooing and their high pH content can damage the hair if not removed or counteracted.

Disease due to animal parasites

Pediculosis (lice)

There are a number of species of lice that particularly affect humans. These parasites need the blood of a host in order to exist.

1. *Pediculus capitis* (head louse) 2mm in length
2. *Pediculus corporus* (body louse)
3. *Phthirus pubis* (crab louse)
4. *Acarus scabiei* (scabies or itch)

Pediculus capitus (the head louse) is very contagious and even fastidiously clean people can become infected, usually through contact with school children. Contrary to what many people think, a head louse does not jump, but transmits itself from head to head by walking. The female lays batches of greyish-white eggs (nits) which attach themselves to the hair shaft near the scalp with a sticky secretion. They are usually found at the sides of the head, behind the ears and in the nape area. One must be particularly tactful when making the client aware that she is infected with lice. It is not necessary for her to see a doctor as she would only be advised to buy the appropriate lotion from the chemist. It is easy to treat the client in the salon. The treatment is relatively simple. Always have the lotion and shampoo available. These contain malathion and carbaryl which effectively kill the lice.

A few simple precautions are necessary when carrying out this treatment. Work with bare arms and, if you have hairy arms, put some lotion on them. Quickly work around the hairline with the lotion then cover the entire scalp, thoroughly saturating the hair. Keep the lotion away from the eyes.

Carbaryl or malathion lotions should be applied to dry hair and then left to dry naturally as the insecticides would be inactivated by any heat. The lotions are a thousand times stronger than the shampoos and will kill lice and eggs in one or two-hour applications, which can be left overnight for about twelve hours to give maximum protection. If there is an infestation in a family, all the family should be treated.

Shampoos have to be used several times to be effective, usually every three days, until the seven to ten days are past. This is the incubation period for eggs. Always use tepid water with the shampoo.

Lotions are generally alcohol-based, but water-based lotions and shampoos are available for those people with a sensitive, broken or eczematous skin or scalp (for whom an alcohol–based lotion would sting), and for asthmatics, babies and young children, to whom the evaporating alcohol may be an irritant. Remember that alcoholic lotions are flammable and should be kept away from naked flame.

The *pediculus corporus, or body louse*, is slightly larger than the head louse but is very similar in appearance. In both cases the males are smaller than the female. The body louse is really a clothing louse and only visits the skin to feed. The eggs are laid in the seams of clothing, especially in underwear nearest to the warmest parts of the body.

Phthiris pubis or crab louse is smaller than the other two and, like the head louse, attaches the eggs to the hair but confines them to the pubic region or short hair on the body.

Acarus scabiei or itch mite causes a disease of the skin called scabies. The parasite burrows in the folds of the skin, usually between the fingers or the front of the wrist, where it lays its eggs. Red spots and lines showing the area of activity. Intense itching and scratching results in spreading the disease to other parts of the body. It is highly contagious and contact with other people should be avoided. Medical advice should be sought as soon as possible.

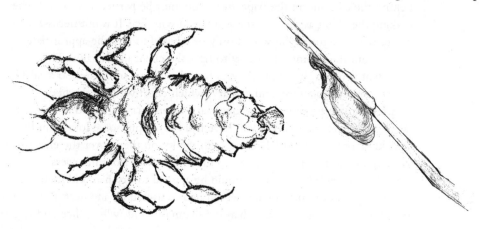

(above left) Pediculosis Capitis (the head louse)
(above right) Pediculosis Capitis (egg or nit attached to a hair)

(right) Scabies (the itch mite)

Protection against germs

First and foremost, it is the doctors and trichologists who must be responsible for the treatment of most skin and scalp disorders, but as hairdressers are in contact with people all the time it is important that you are able to recognize the common skin disorders on the heads of clients, and take precautions to help prevent the spread of infection.

Bacteria, the micro-organisms that spread infection, can be found everywhere. The skin, unbroken and intact, can be a great protection against germs falling on its surface. This is because the skin has an 'acid mantle' or surface film made of a mixture of oil, sebum and sweat. This mixture is slightly acid, with pH 4.2 to 5.6, which can also neutralize small amounts of alkali. Sweat, too, is acid at pH 4 to 6.8 (pH 7 is neutral).

Streptococci germs, which can be carried in the throat, can cause scarlet fever, erysipelas, impetigo and other serious illnesses. Staphylococci germs, which are often present on the skin, cause abscesses, boils, impetigo, folliculitis and infected dermatitis. The 'acid mantle' can destroy the streptococci germs, but it cannot destroy staphylococci . These germs thrive in any break in the skin's surface from which any tiny flow of serum leaks, such as cracks in the skin, abrasions, slight cuts or scratch marks. Thorough washing with soap and water will remove them, so too will the natural peeling of the skin. This is why hygiene should be made a priority in all salon procedures, from shampooing onwards, and whenever contact is made with the scalp or hair.

Germs can be transferred to the face and hands, to handkerchiefs, to towels and gowns, and thus on to other people if sensible hygienic precautions are not taken.

Not all diseases are caused by bacteria, there are other organisms such as viruses and fungi.

Viruses are minute but can only reproduce in the cells of other organisms. Like parasites, they use the host cells' metabolism for their own reproduction. Virus infections include shingles, poliomyelitis, warts, verrucae and smallpox.

Fungi are microscopic plant organisms made up of many cells. They act as parasites (live on living matter) or can be saprophytes (live on decaying or dead matter).

Tinea capitis (ringworm of the scalp) is a disease caused by a fungal infection producing red pimples or patches at the opening of the hair follicle. The patches can spread and the hair becomes brittle and falls out. It is extremely contagious and no person with this condition should use any salon services but should be treated by a doctor.

With so many germs and harmful organisms around us every day it is a wonder that people are not permanently ailing, but most people develop some natural immunity to most ills. This can be built up by having a balanced daily routine of proper nourishment, rest and personal hygiene to keep the body functioning well. The body will always use its own defence mechanism and, provided a person is healthy, the first line of defence is an unbroken skin.

Conclusion

To be a true craftsman it is necessary to have a sound knowledge of the basic hairdressing skills. You must become familiar with all the tools and their uses and be able to manipulate them in a comfortable and relaxed manner, and you must have an instinctive feel for line and design.

Line is a word that has become part of the hairdressing vocabulary, but what does it mean? To me it is the design, shape, direction and movement of a style! It is not rigid; it must flow; it must have blended movement and balance; it must be completely sympathetic to a woman's personality and to the many facets of her features so that the hairstyle is an inspired creation with line, shape and balance. Feeling is something that cannot be taught; it must come from within. It is this which makes you aware of fashion, and enables you to create styles that can adapted artistically and commercially to suit the current trends. Never be afraid of fashion: it is only a variation of length and shape in hair, just as with clothes it is the length of a skirt, the width of a lapel, or the billow of a sleeve. Similarly, in music, a basic theme is taken and played in the most intriguing variations. Everything seems to return in cycles, whether it is in music, art, clothes or hairdressing; the basic concepts are taken up, re-used, turned around and presented again.

During my teaching and lecturing career, both here and abroad, I have found many people who appear to be searching for some magical secret in hairdressing – cutting especially. But the only secret is learning the basics and sticking to the rules from the very beginning. The creation of a simple line with shape and balance are the aims of a true artist. It is this which I have tried to illustrate in this book.

Silvio Camillo

'Everything in nature is curved and if God had intended women to have square breasts, he would have made them that way.'

Glossary of hairdressing terms

Acid rinse
Containing properties to close the cuticle of the hair, also to neutralize alkalinity.

Acid mantle
A mixture of oil–sweat–sebum collected on the surface of the skin as a film.

Allergy
A reaction to contact with something, usually seen as dermatitis on the skin in hairdressing.

Alopecia
Medical name for baldness. There are various kinds of alopecia.

Alpha-keratin
Hair in its unstretched state.

Amino acids
Proteins within the cortex of hair.

Ammonium thioglycollate
The salt which is the main ingredient of most cold wave solutions.

Anagen
The growing stage of hair.

Asymmetrical
Not evenly balanced, but offset to one side.

Azo-dyes
Some of the semi-permanent perming lotions contain these dyes.

Back-brushing
Achieving volume and support to hair shape by a series of pushing strokes into the root with the brush.

Back-combing
A similar technique to back-brushing but using the comb.

Balance
A term used to describe the line and shape of a hair style in relation to the face and body.

Baldness
The loss of hair on the head; medical name alopecia.

Barrier cream
A cream to protect the hands and the skin.

Base colour
The natural colour of the hair.

Binding or back-binding
Fluffing up the hair along a mesh with the brush to provide body.

Bleaching
A process of lightening the natural colour of the hair.

Blended wave movement
Describes the shadow-waved shaped on the crown which joins the waved shape from the small side of the parting to the large side.

Blow-waving or blow-drying
Styling the hair in a certain pattern with the hand dryer and a brush.

Braiding
The plaiting of hair.

Brightening shampoo
Specially prepared shampoos to lighten the base colour of the hair by one or two shades.

Brushing
The most important technique in preparing the dressing-out stage of a hair style, not just to loosen hair.

Buckled roots
Misshapen and bent hair at the roots caused by hair not being combed properly.

Buckled points
Bent hair ends: can be caused by 'frizziness' through careless rollering.

Camomile
Vegetable colorant made from flowers of camomile plant, often found in blonde rinses.

Canities
Greying of hair: lack of colouring pigment in the hair.

Cape
A protective covering for the client's shoulders.

Capillary
Small blood vessels that supply the hair follicle with its oxygen and growth.

Carbuncle
A number of septic hair follicles together.

Cascade
A fall of hair shape on any part of the head.

Catogen
The period in which the hair starts to deteriorate and begins to break up.

Caucasian
White or European hair

Caustic
A strong alkali that can damage other substances and also skin and hair. It is used in curl relaxers.

Citric acid
Acid found in citrus fruits, used in acid rinses to counteract alkalinity and to close the cuticle of the hair.

Clipper
Tool used to graduate the nape; used mainly in male hairdressing.

Clips
Used in setting to fix pin-curls in place: also to control barrel-curls at the base.

Club cutting (blunt cutting)
Cutting which produces a straight bevel on the ends of the hair.

Cohesive set
Wetting of hair, moulding and drying in stretched placing, e.g. as in shampoo and set.

Coif
A small close-fitting cap or bonnet. The words 'Coiffure' and 'Coiffeur' are derived from it.

Coiffeur and coiffeuse
Masculine and feminine words for 'Hairdresser' (French). Hairdressing as a

separate occupation, apart from the trade of Barber–Surgeon, did not exist before the 17th century. Before that time women depended upon their maids for this service.

Cold waving
A method of imparting a movement or curl to human hair by means of a chemical solution. A series of complicated changes in the molecular structure of the hair take place during this processing. Subsequently the hair is normalized, fixing the hair permanently in its new curled formation.

Conditioner
A substance to improve and protect the condition of hair. There are also penetrating conditioners that can open the cuticle and act from within.

Contagious
Transmission of disease by contact with a person suffering from it.

Cortex
The middle part of the hair containing the fibrils and micro–fibrils, the essential strength of the hair and also the melanin, the natural colour of the hair.

Crescent curl
A long stem with the points softly turned.

Crest
The top ridge of a wave between two troughs or hollows.

Crimping
Deliberate distortion or frizzing of hair.

Croquignole
Winding from point into the roots (derived from French).

Crown
The top part of the head: its shape usually dictates the natural fall of the hair.

Curl base
The scalp end of the curl.

Curl stem
The section between the base and the points.

Cuticle
The outer layer of the hair.

Cutting angle
Angle in which the hair is held and the direction in which the scissors make the cut.

Cyst
A fluid-filled sac on the head caused by the blocking of a duct from the sebaceous gland to the follicle.

Cystine
An amino acid found in plants and animals. It is an essential part of the keratins of the human body, such as hair and nails, and therefore vital to their growth.

Dandruff
Dried skin scales seen on the scalp - also known as pityriasis.

Decolouring
Reducing colour from hair that is too dark, by applying decolorant to the parts of the hair where colour build-up has occurred.

Density
Thickness of the hair which may be fine, medium, heavy, coarse or abundant.

Depilatory
Product that is used to remove unwanted hair from face, arms and legs. Care is necessary to avoid damage to the skin.

Depth
Depth of the wave, the movement or the cut.

Dermal papilla
The cells at the base of the hair follicle from which the hair is formed.

Dermatitis
An inflammation of the skin caused by irritation from some external (or even internal) means. The condition can appear in a dry, wet or moist form; it can be caused by careless use of perm lotion.

Dermis
The true skin or layer of skin beneath the outer skin or epidermis from which it is divided by the basal layer: the part of the scalp and body covering containing blood vessels, nerve endings and sweat glands, composed of fine strands of elastic tissue upon which allow the body covering to expand and contract.

Detergent
A class of substances that will free other substances from dirt, grease and other debris. Soapless preparations are detergents, so are cleansing lotions.

Development
In a permanent wave, 'development' means the degree of elasticity and tension produced in the wave movement; affected by time and temperature. In colour, it is the depth of colour achieved in a hair colouring process; also affected by time.

Diagnosis
In hairdressing, this is the analysis of the scalp before any hairdressing procedure is carried out.

Disease
Any alteration of the normal vital processes of the body. Disease of the scalp and hair may be due to chemical or physical irritants, animal parasites, organism or bacteria.

Disentangle
Removing tangles and frizzed hair, usually with wide-toothed comb.

Disinfectant
Substance or chemical which is germicidal (lethal to micro-organisms).

Distortions
Twisted growth of hair in various directions on the crown or at the hair line.

Disulphide bonds
These are the strongest bonds within the cortex of the hair.

Dressing-out
The final presentation or comb-out after a set, using comb or brush techniques.

Eczema
A condition where the skin is inflamed and there is an eruption or rash.

Effleurage
A smoothing massage movement.

Elasticity
The manner in which hair can be stretched and returned to its original length.

Electrolysis
System used in hairdressing for the destruction of superfluous hair.

Emulsion bleach
A type of bleach used for lightening hair.

End papers
Used to prevent distorted and buckled points of the hair when winding a perm.

Ends
The points of the hair or the last inch from the scalp.

Epilation
Technical term denoting plucking.

European hair
Describes hair of people of European origin – Caucasian hair.

Exclamation hairs
The characteristic shape of hairs affected by alopecia areata.

Exothermic
A chemical reaction in which heat is given off.

Finger wave
Method of patterning the head in a waved shape using the fingers and comb.

Fish hooks
Twisted points of the hair caused through bad winding.

Foil strips
Strips of specially prepared foil (aluminium) used in bleaching procedures such as weave-highlights.

Follicle
A downward growth into the dermis.

Folliculitis
Infection of the hair follicle.

Fragilitas crinium
Term used to define broken and split ends caused by harsh hair treatment.

French pleat
Where the back hair is manipulated and pinned into a fold from the nape towards the crown.

Frizz
Hair that is tightly curled at the ends.

Gel
A thick emulsion used to style and fix certain effects in hair.

Geometric
In hairdressing: hair cut to a pattern which is square, angular or triangular with the ends cut evenly and solid with no layering.

Germicide
Substance that can kill and inhibit the growth of micro-organisms.

Glands
An organ secreting certain constituents from the body, e.g. sebaceous gland or sweat glands. The sebaceous gland produces 'sebum' the natural oil of the skin and hair.

Graduation
Hair that is cut short at the nape but in longer lengths further up. It can also denote blending the longer lengths with shorter lengths anywhere on the head.

Grecian style
A knot of hair either on the crown or at the back of the head, secured with a pin and with the ends waved or curled.

Growth
Direction in which the hair is growing: growth distortions include circular and half-circular twists, sometimes called 'whorls' and 'half-whorls'.

Guideline
The initial cutting procedure around the perimeter of the head that provides a cutting line to follow when layering a cut.

Hair line
The edge of the growing hair, at the forehead, around the ear and into the nape.

Hair
Filaments growing from the skin, especially of the human body: the last of the tissues to yield to decay. Consists chemically of about one-half carbon,

one-fifth nitrogen, one-fifth oxygen, one-twentieth hydrogen, one-twentieth sulphur. Proportions vary according to colour.

Hair-growth cycle
The three stages of the growth of hair: anagen, catagen, telogen.

Half-shaft
The part of the hair projecting from the follicle in the skin.

Haute coiffure
The highest standard in hair design.

Head louse (pediculosis capitis)
Insect that infests the head and hair and lays eggs called nits.

Henna
A red colouring derived from the Egyptian privet used on the hair. It is incompatible with permanent waving lotions.

Hirsute
Abnormal hair growth.

Horny layer
This is the first layer of the skin (epidermis) and mostly consists of dead cells which are shed through the skin.

Hydrogen peroxide
An oxidizing agent found in many neutralizers and bleaches and mixed with tints.

Incompatibility
When substances do not mix together they are said to be incompatible, i.e. water and oil. In hairdressing an incompatibility test can determine whether the hair would be damaged by the use of any product.

Infestation
Being overrun or plagued by creatures, insects, etc. A person's hair may be infested by lice.

Inflammation
A reaction to some form of irritant which shows as an area of redness.

Inversion
In haircutting, a term used to describe an inward 'V' movement.

Keratin
Horny substance forming hair, nails, feathers and hooves. There are different forms of keratin: the horny structure of hair is quite different from that of a toenail.

Kink
A mark caused on the hair shaft by a badly placed elastic during permanent waving.

Lacquer
Used principally to fix a hair style, giving a protective transparent covering which dries immediately on spraying. It can easily be removed by combing and shampooing with soapless shampoo.

Lanugo hair
Associated with the hair found on a premature baby. Is often descriptive of the very soft, fine, downy colourless hair that gives the female skin its soft, velvety quality.

Layering
A method of cutting and blending various lengths of hair throughout the head.

Lice (pediculus capitis)
An infestation of the hair on the head, usually accompanied by intense itching and scratching. The three types of lice can be killed with special lotions.

Lightener
Used to lift the colour of hair one or two shades, often as lightening shampoo.

Liquid bleach
A mixture of ammonium hydroxide and hydrogen peroxide.

Lotions
Liquid preparations generally containing water and alcohol mixed with various drugs and chemicals used as stimulating scalp preparations. Some of the chemical-containing liquids used in permanent waving are sometimes referred to as lotions but are technically named solutions or reagents.

Lowlights
Small meshes of hair coloured darker than the base colour of the hair.

Male pattern baldness
The usual receding pattern of baldness at the temples and crown in men.

Manicure
The professional treatment for hands and nails.

Marcel wave
Method of permanent waving using curling irons, invented by Marcel Gratten.

Massage
Manipulation of the scalp or body by scientific application of certain hand and finger movements (derived from the French 'masser' – to knead).

Medicated shampoo
A specially prepared shampoo containing medication for use in the extreme cases of dandruff.

Medulla
The centre portion of the hair shaft. It is the least important part of the hair and, in some hairs, it is not present. It does not appear in lanugo hair.

Melanin
The name given to the colouring matter present in normal skin and hair. The substance is manufactured naturally, when natural or artificial sunlight comes into contact with the skin and forms a protective barrier of pigment.

Mesh
A small section or division of hair.

Micro-layering
A method of invisibly layering the hair with a special technique using the razor.

Mongoloid
Straight, lank hair from Eastern countries.

Monilethrix
An abnormality of the hair shaft which is alternately swollen and beaded along the length.

Mousse
A creamy type of foam product used as a setting agent or for temporary colouring.

Nape
The neck just underneath the occipital bone at the back of the head.

Nape line or Neck line
Neck lines have characteristics, just like faces. They can be short, long, full, narrow, wide, etc. The neck line needs to be studied carefully to balance the hairstyle.

Nape hair
Base hair from which all graduated cutting starts upwards.

Net
A fine material knotted into a fine mesh, used to cover the setting rollers before placing the client under the dryer.

Neutrality
Chemical term describing a state which is neither acid nor alkaline.

Neutralization
The process whereby the acidity or alkalinity of a solution is counteracted by the addition of alkali or acid in exactly sufficient quantity to produce neutrality.

Neutralizing
(In perming) fixing the wave movement by a chemical process.

Nit
The eggs of the head louse (pediculus capitis) usually found stuck to the hair near the scalp, behind the ears or in the occipital region of the head.

Nitro-dye
Used in semi-permanent colouring.

Normalizing
Another word used to describe neutralizing chemically processed hair (permanent wave).

Occipital
The bone at the base of the skull at the back of the head.

Oil bleach
A type of hair lightener in the form of an oil.

Oils
There is a large variety of natural and manufactured oils divisible into three main groups, essential oils, fixed oils and mineral oils.

Outline
The start of a cut – outline or perimeter of a head.

Overlapping
Applying solution to the previously tinted or bleached hair, instead of keeping to the untreated regrowth.

Oxidation, oxidization
The act of combining oxygen with another substance.

Papilla
Contained small growth from which the hair grows at the base of the hair follicle in the dermis.

Para dye
A permanent colouring made from the small molecule 'para-dyes', i.e. Paraphenylediamine, which are known as penetrating oxidization dyes.

Patch test
Commonly used for 'skin test' or pre-disposition test, to determine any sensitivity to chemicals or tinting procedure.

Permanent waving
A chemical process which alters the structure of the hair by breaking the disulphide bonds within the cortex and then fixing them in their new formation around the curlers.

Petrissage
Deep massaging movement used in general massage.

pH number
Defines the degree of acidity or alkalinity of solution.

Pin-curls
A way of setting small meshes of hair with the points curved inwards towards the scalp and secured with a double clip.

Pityriasis (Capitex simplex)
Dandruff. An inflammation of the skin, forming the flaking of fine bran-like scales.

Pivot-point
Defines the point, usually on the crown of the head, from which movement is directed during the cutting of a style.

Pompadour
A type of styling with the hair brushed up from the forehead. Madame Pompadour was Mistress of Louis XV of France.

Pre-pigmentate
Adding of colour to hair before tinting because of colour fading,

Premature greyness
A hereditary complaint that usually runs in families.

Protofibrils
Contained within the cortex of the hair.

Psoriasis
A skin disease which is non-infectious but can be quite unpleasant in some cases. Seen on the scalp as thick circular silvery lesions of skin, often inflamed around the edges.

Reagent
A substance used to bring about a permanent waving process on hair; also known as a solution and a lotion.

Reduction dye
To reduce unwanted colour from hair, also known as a stripper.

Regrowth
New growth nearest the scalp that has to be tinted or bleached.

Restructurant
A conditioning treatment that works from within the inner structure of the hair.

Reverse-curl setting
A manner of placing pin-curls or rollers in alternate rows, clockwise and anti-clockwise, to achieve a waved shape.

Ringed hair
An unusual condition caused at birth through a malfunction in the cortex giving the hair an opaque look. Parts of the pigment are hidden.

Ringworm (Tinea)
A fungal skin disease which can affect any part of the body. The scalp and hair is affected by rounded, scaly partially-bald spots with an outer reddish ring. Remaining hairs are short, broken and twisted stumps.

Root
Cells holding the hair in a follicle.

Scalp
The skin covering of the cranium.

Scissors
A tool for cutting hair.

Sebaceous gland
Gland attached to the hair follicle in the last layer of the dermis.

Seborrhoea
An oily condition caused by an over-active sebaceous gland. It can also cause S.Sicc which is an accumulation of greasy scales or crusts and S. capitis of the scalp, commonly called dandruff or pytriasis.

Sebum
Fatty oily secretion of the sebaceous gland.

Sensitivity test
Test to find out whether a person is allergic to certain chemicals or conditions, e.g. in tinting.

Setting (Mis-en-plis)
Pattern of rollers or pin-curls used to achieve a hairdressing shape.

Shingle
Cutting the hair short close to the nape of the neck and gradually longer towards the crown.

Slithering
Tapering the hair to graduated lengths with a slithering stroke action using a half-closed blade of the scissors.

Soap scum
A residue left on the scalp, usually after shampooing in hard water etc. An acetic acid rinse will clear the scalp.

Solution
A liquid in which has been dissolved other substances. Lotions used in permanent waving are known as a solutions or reagents.

Spiral winding
Winding from the root to the points in permanent waving.

Steamer
An apparatus much resembling a hair dryer producing a gentle flow of steam, used in hair reconditioning treatments.

Straightening
Taking movement or curl out of hair: also known as relaxing.

Strand test
A preliminary test given before any hairdressing process to determine the degree of porosity or elasticity of the hair as well as the ability of the hair to withstand the effects of chemicals.

Streaking
Lightening tiny meshes of hair around the hairline and front of the head attractively to contrast with the base colour of the hair.

Swirl
The stroke or formation of a large half-circled movement at the back of the head.

Switch
A long weft of hair, tail-like with a loop moulded at the end.

Symmetrical
Evenly balanced hair shape, with equal proportions on both sides of the head.

Tail comb
A half-comb with a handle tapering to a point.

Tapering
Removing some of the density of hair and length using scissors or razor cutting to a point.

Teasing
A slight back-combing of the hair while dressing-out: a light fluffing action that puffs out the hair, sometimes called French lacing.

Telegen
A resting stage of the hair growth cycle.

Temporal bone
The two bones at either side of the head, just above the ears, and between the frontal and the occipital bone at the back of the head.

Temporary colour
A temporary hair colour that usually lasts between shampoos.

Terminal hair
The coarse hair found on the body.

Test cutting
To determine the reaction of a sample mesh of hair to colouring and breakage.

Test curl
To determine how a client's hair will react to a permanent wave solution and processing.

Texture
Of hair – the general quality as to coarse, medium, fine; the feel of the hair, its elasticity, strength or lankness.

Thermostat
Switch that automatically regulates and controls the temperature.

Thinning
Removing thickness of the hair without losing any length.

Thio
The chemical ammonium thioglycollate used in permanent waving.

Tinea
The medical term for Ringworm.

Tinting
In hairdressing – to colour the hair with a permanent hair tint, a temporary colouring or colour rinse.

Tone
The intensity, depth of a colour, e.g. red, blonde, ash, etc.

Toner
A special colorant that is applied to lightened hair to lose unwanted tones and achieve a true delicate colouring.

Toupee
A small wig used to cover the top of the head.

Traction alopecia
Baldness that happens when there is excessive pull at the roots, causing it to loosen the hair follicle and fall out.

Transformation
A semi-wig, an artificial covering of hair for the front, sides and back of the head, but with no crown. The long hair covers the crown and mingles with the natural hair.

Trichologist
The qualified trichologist is trained in the diagnosis of hair, skin and scalp diseases and in the correct treatment of such disorders with whatever medicines and remedies necessary.

Trichology
The science of the care of the hair and scalp. From the Greek 'trichos' meaning hair.

Trichonodosis
Knotted hair.

Trichotillomania
A condition which produces a form of incomplete alopecia. Patients are invariably subjects who pull out their own hair until they produce a bald patch.

Trough
The dip or hollow of the wave.

Twist
A term used in spiral winding in permanent waving. The hair is wound flatly as any twisting of the mesh would result in a distorted curl and wave.

Under-developed
Insufficiently processed, e.g. as in bleaching.

Under-processed
Incorrect timing during the permanent waving period so that, within the cortex of the hair, insufficient bonds have been broken.

Undulation
The wave shape.

Unevenness
Hair colour that does not show the true colour throughout the head.

Vegetable colouring
Hair colorant derived from plants and vegetables, e.g. camomile, henna.

Vellus hair
Soft downy hair found on the body.

Water-softener
Certain chemicals such as the carbonate or phosphate of sodium used to soften hard water will permit lathering with shampoo and soap.

Wave, Cold
A system of permanently waving the hair without using heat.

Wave, Permanent
Processing the hair so that the wave is permanent.

Wave, Thermal
A wave put in the hair with heated irons or tongs.

Weft
An artificial section of woven hair used for practice or as a substitute for natural hair.

White hair
A form of canities where the hair has lost its natural colour. It can appear prematurely as a white streak in both male and females heads and can also be hereditary.

Whorl
A hair whorl or cow's lick is a spiral turn causing a tuft of hair to lie contrary to the natural fall.

Wig
An artificial covering for the head consisting of a network of interwoven hair.

Wiglet
A flat based hairpiece used to cover small bald areas of the head.

Winding, Croquignole
Winding the hair points towards the scalp.

Winding, Spiral
Winding from the scalp towards the points resulting in a ringlet type of curl.

Wrapping
A method of wrapping the hair around the head and drying, then repeating the process wrapping it the opposite way: used to straighten wavy hair.

Yak hair
Soft, silky hair of the Tibetan yak, used by wigmakers in special wigs to strengthen human hair wigs, but used particularly for theatrical wigs, especially white dress wigs.

Index